The Remarkable Trees of St Albans Revisited

by

Kate Bretherton

Main photographs by
Donato Cinicolo

KATE BRETHERTON
Flint Barn, Norrington End, Redding Lane, Redbourn, AL3 7QN;
kate@hellotrees.co.uk; www.hellotrees.co.uk

Information on this title: as above or info@hellotrees.co.uk

Published by Kate Bretherton

First published 2018 as an update of 'The Remarkable Trees of St Albans' published
in 2010

Typeset by Flower Typesetting (jane.a.flower@gmail.com)

Printed through SS Media Limited: Cardinal Point, Park Road, Rickmansworth,
Hertfordshire WD3 1RE; info@ss-media.co.uk; www.ss-media.co.uk.

A catalogue record for this publication is available from the British Library

ISBN 978-0-9927994-6-5

Front cover illustration: Princess Diana's cedar at the north east corner of St Albans
Abbey.

Back cover illustration: Fallen woodland leaves in Autumn.

Contents

Foreword

Trees are one of the most important natural elements within the urban landscape of the City and District of St Albans. Whether appearing individually, in groups or as woodlands, trees are essential to life and their value cannot be overstated. They:

- are an important part of the landscape and contribute to people's quality of life and sense of well being;
- release oxygen for us to breathe;
- absorb carbon dioxide (thereby reducing the greenhouse effect);
- filter air and reduce other pollutants such as ozone, nitrogen oxides, sulphur dioxides, carbon monoxide, smoke, dust and ash;
- increase biodiversity by providing a variety of habitats for wildlife – a mature tree can provide support for over 460 different species of mammals, birds and insects;
- provide a renewable resource of timber, fruit, seeds, nuts and fuel;
- create aesthetic value, improving the appearance of our environment by providing a variety of scale, form, colour and shape;
- reduce wind speeds, giving shelter and comfort;
- reduce noise levels;
- reduce flash flooding;
- reduce everyday stress, particularly important in today's environment – research has shown that hospital patients recover more quickly when able to enjoy the view of trees;
- provide shade from the sun and make areas more attractive to live and work in;
- positively affect property values and help to attract investment.

David Curry
October 2010

Opposite: An ancient beech in the Abbey churchyard in the heart of town reminds us of how much less our lives would without trees

Preface to the Remarkable Trees of St Albans Revisited

'The Remarkable Trees of St Albans' was a remarkable success; all 1000 copies were sold out within 14 months of publication in November 2010.

The success was partly due to the book being a good present. Donato Cinicolo's photographs are wonderful and people like trees: they provide us with oxygen, are beautiful and lift our spirits. What's not to like.

Particularly encouraging comments I received were that the book has made readers more aware of our trees, that looking up at them lifts their spirits, and bringing to mind the stories associated with the trees has been life enhancing. I liked, too, to hear that readers have gone back to the book to find out more and have used it when taking children to parks.

Since the book sold out, I have been asked by both St Albans Civic Society and the Arc & Arc (St Albans and Hertfordshire Architectural and Archaeological Society) to arrange for a reprint.

I have kept the original as a snapshot of trees in 2010. Where there is more to say, I put a number (N) next to that topic and added a note against that number at the end of each chapter. I have also added an index.

I have not recorded every tree that has died or new ones planted, even when I have known about them – only if they are interesting in some way.

I hope you enjoy the update.

Acknowledgements again

In producing 'The Remarkable Trees of St Albans Revisited', I had invaluable help in copy editing and/or fact checking from Peter Burley, Peter Crick, Maggy and Roderick Douglas, Ruth Jeavens, Patrick McNeill, Jon Mein and Roger Miles.

'It is the photographs that make it, of course,' everyone says. They do indeed. Thank you, Donato, from all of us.

Opposite:
A woodland
path

Preface

Are the trees in this book remarkable?

Some are remarkable in the way in which we would expect: they are old or rare or of exceptional beauty.

Many trees have none of these characteristics but someone in our community finds them remarkable for their associations – the memories or ideas that the tree evokes. Where people have been willing to share these associations with us, their trees have been included and I hope you will enjoy their stories as much as I have done.

I would also say that St Albans District's trees as a whole are remarkable: we are rich in specimen trees, in native woodlands, trees in streets, parks and churchyards.

Photographs can sometimes change our perception and, if anyone's photographs can do that, Donato Cinicolo's can. Then, having seen the photograph, or heard of an interesting association, there is the different experience of seeing the tree for oneself, being near the tree, being under its branches. I hope this book will lead you to new awareness, new experiences and an increased enjoyment of the wonderful trees around us.

Acknowledgements

This book was produced under the auspices of St Albans District Council Tree Warden Scheme. My thanks go to David Curry, Co-ordinator of the Tree Warden Scheme for his steady mentoring through the whole challenging process; to all those people who told us of their favourite trees - or trees that needed to be included in a book about St Albans trees; to Donato Cinicolo for his wonderful photographs – and for making our expeditions to find the trees such enjoyable adventures; to Anne Valentine for convincing me that, to do a proper job, I needed professional page layout and proof reading; to Jane Flower of Flower Typesetting for setting out the pages so attractively and coping with all the implications of my being a novice author and publisher; to Chris Pudsey for doing a combined editing and proof-reading job to a tight deadline; and to my friends for their tolerance and support while I have been obsessed with the book.

Kate Bretherton
October 2010

Opposite:
ander's Mexican
me in Camp
Road is a
remarkable tree
n every way: it
s rare, ancient,
magnificent,
beautiful and has
n interesting
istory

Paul Arnold's trees planted for their historical connections

When Paul Arnold(1) told me about the trees he had planted for their historical connections, I wanted everyone interested in St Albans now and in the future to know about them – and that is how this book came to be written.

The project has widened to include trees in our parks and streets, people's specific favourites and some issues to do with trees, but it is Paul's trees and how they came to be planted that have been my inspiration.

Paul had been a forester in Lincolnshire and in Hertfordshire and came to work for St Albans City Parks Department in the 1970s. Once it occurred to him to plant trees for their historical connections, he came up with all sorts of ideas. The trees that resulted are a life-enhancing legacy for us all.

This opening chapter is what Paul Arnold told me about his trees.

Opposite: Paul Arnold in 2010

Right: Paul's ecumenical holm oak

The French connection

Paul Arnold's project of planting trees for their historical connections started when the St Albans Civic Society was concerned about 'the dreadful state' of the area where the drinking fountain used to be between the Clock Tower and the High Street at the end of French Row.

Council departments, Paul tells us, were often under fire from the Civic Society so he thought it was astute of Mr Plant, Head of the Parks Department at the time, to suggest to them that they design the layout and the Parks Department would put it into effect. This turned out to be a good idea because even within the Society there was considerable disagreement and the Parks people were glad to be out of the politics.

The layout included a circle of benches and shaped paving stones to represent three circular landmarks that had been on this site: the 13th century Eleanor Cross, the 18th century Market Cross and water pump, and the 19th century drinking fountain. The layout also included a tree.

Initially, the tree was to be positioned close to the Great Red Lion (now Zizzi's) – too close for the Parks Department because, by then, the effects of trees on building subsidence was beginning to be understood. The Civic Society agreed to a new position a little further from the buildings.

What sort of tree should they plant? The adjacent French Row made Paul Arnold think of the famous French gardener Jean Robin and the tree named after him, the robinia. Paul had made his first historical connection.

It is in Jean Robin's gardens at the French Court of Henry IV and Louis XIII that the tree is first known in Europe, and it was through Robin's friendship and collaboration with John Tradescant the Elder that the robinia was introduced to this country. John Tradescant was employed by the Cecil family at Theobald Palace and then at nearby Hatfield House. The jaunty image of a gardener in knee-length puffed-out trousers and tall hat carved into the great staircase of the house is thought to be a portrait of John Tradescant the Elder.

The robinia has light and airy leaves and lovely upward-reaching, zig-zagging branches(2).

The bark is deeply grooved and, with age, becomes gnarled and interestingly weird.

The flowers are white and clustered in cascades. I saw a young woman cup a cascade in her two hands and draw it against her cheek. It was a precious moment.

Robinia flowers

A single robinia flower

Do the flowers remind you of sweet pea or runner bean flowers? They are all in the same family and used to be called Leguminosae but are now Fabaciae.

The robinia is a native of North America and its common names are false acacia, locust tree and black locust. Mimosa trees, which grow in Australia and Africa, are real acacias. They have more feathery leaves than the robinia but are also Fabaciae.

But why do you think the robinia is called a locust tree? The story is stranger than fiction.

At the end of French Row a robinia was planted for its French connection

Early Pilgrim Fathers knew the Bible story of John the Baptist being sustained by locusts when he dwelt in the wilderness, but they also thought that it was not really insects but carob pods that he ate, so, when they saw a tree with what looked like carob pods, they called it a locust tree. What is truly brilliant

A robinia pod

fun is that there is no ambiguity about the meaning of the original word used, and scholars now accept that the Gospels tell us that St John ate locust insects. The current Greek word for locust, *akris*, was sometimes used in the ancient world to mean carob, which is presumably the origin of the confusion, but my guess is that it caught on because squeamish Westerners did not like the idea of their saint doing anything as 'primitive' as eating insects.

Unfortunately the robinia pods have nothing like the chocolate-flavoured sticky pulp found round carob seeds.

And what of French Row and its French connection? A shiny black board(3) outside the Fleur de Lys tells us that John, King of France, when he was captured after the Battle of Poitiers in 1356, was held in a building on this site. However, the illustrated board at the entrance to the side passage casts doubt on King John of France ever having been held here in French Row.

Rather than King John of France staying here, it might have been a group of French mercenaries recruited by the barons more than a century earlier in 1216 to help curb our own bad King John.

There is certainly a tradition(4) of a French connection here – the name of the passage commemorates it – and it is right that a tree should do the same.

Information on a board close by casts doubt on King John of France having been held in French Row

Verdun(5): the last tree left standing

The St Albans City Parks Department started to purchase trees in containers and their supplier was a Surrey nursery where a nurseryman had been over to France to the battlefield of Verdun(6) and brought back some conkers from the only tree, a horsechestnut, left standing after the battle.

When Paul Arnold, on a trip to the nursery, heard the story he asked for one of the seedlings. The nurseryman had a habit of planting seeds in obsolete metal milk crates and that is probably where our conker started its life. A City Guide told me that she had often wondered why the Battle of Verdun, very much a French-German battle, had been chosen to be commemorated in St Albans. It was the result of a coincidence.

On his return, Paul selected a place for the sapling in Waxhouse Gate and contacted the British Legion in St Albans. There was a surviving 'Old Contemptible' among their membership and it was he(7) who planted the tree on the anniversary of Verdun to commemorate the battle and in memory of the men who lost their lives.

'Old Contemptible' was the title proudly adopted by the men of the British Expeditionary Force who saw service before or on 22nd November 1914. They derive their title from the famous Order of the Day given by Kaiser Wilhelm II on 19 August 1914 '... to walk over General French's contemptible little Army'. This is obviously a translation, but the irony of the derogatory term is inescapable: these were brave and tenacious men, the first of an army that was – eventually and after tragic losses – victorious.

A sombre occasion to commemorate all those lost at the Battle of Verdun

For many decades, all survivors of the First World War were honoured with the title, but by the time we were down to only a very few survivors, we seemed no longer willing to use the term, even in conscious irony.

I pictured the Battle of Verdun being fought across a field and lasting for some days. The battle took place over more than 60 square miles; fierce bombardment and hand-to-hand fighting lasted for 10 months and skirmishes continued for another 2 years.

The opening attack on 21 February 1916 was from a barrage of 1,400 guns ranged over 8 miles.

The equivalent, if St Albans were the objective, would be fire from a line of 1,400 guns – mortars – from Harpenden to Welwyn Garden City trained on our defences dotted around the villages in between, smashing through homes, pubs, churches, woodlands, into hillsides, sending mud flying everywhere and creating a quagmire and heaps of rubble and timber.

The town of Verdun has a citadel within it and to the north east of the town and east of the River Meuse there was a network of 18 forts with passages below ground and turrets with rotating artillery above but, by 1916, a good deal of the artillery had been taken from Verdun forts to be used elsewhere leaving the area vulnerable.

Maps of the battle show wiggling lines of the German advance towards Verdun with labels '24 Feb', '9 April', '8 Aug'. Fort after fort was taken, many of them hard won with fighting day after day, barricade by barricade, sometimes in narrow underground corridors.

Both sides suffered terribly. '*Ils ne passeront pas!*' was General Robert Nivelle's official order of the day on 23 June 1916. The expression has become a byword for French resolve, and Verdun a byword for French tenacity.

So, of what relevance is this tragic battle to Britain and St Albans?

The French defence of Verdun meant that the Kaiser had depleted resources to withstand the Russian attack on his Eastern Front in the late summer of 1916.

Verdun meant that the Kaiser did not reach Paris. Nor win the war.

Our Verdun horsechestnut is tall and beautiful

In late March, from each sticky bud formed the previous autumn, comes leaf after leaf, a flower bud, and more leaves, each leaf large and palmate. It is like a magician producing strings of silk handkerchiefs out of a hat – only here the hat is as small as the top of my finger and the handkerchiefs bigger than my hands. The leaves are cream-coloured and furry at first, swelling into a wholesome green palmate shape of up to seven leaflets.

Opposite: The horsechestnut planted for the Battle of Verdun

Masses of flowers open soon after the leaves. They appear in clusters, panicles, that look like candles. Each panicle is made up of up to 40 pink-spotted(8), five-petalled flowers.

Then the tree seems to relax into its own spreading beauty for the summer, the insect-pollinated flowers mutating into mahogany-glossy conkers, each in its round spiny green case.

Horsechestnut flowers

In autumn, each leaf(9) takes on more than one colour: shades of reds and browns and oranges and vestigial greens. And, long before the leaves are ready to drop, the distinctive sticky buds that hold next year's leaves and flowers begin to appear.

There is another reason that a horsechestnut is an appropriate tree to represent a battle. In both world wars, the starch from conkers was used to produce acetone required to gelatinise the mixture of guncotton, nitroglycerine and petroleum jelly that makes up cordite, an almost smokeless explosive. Crown Prince Wilhelm, on that first day alone of the battle, fired 100,000 shells an hour for 21 hours into the French defences. The fact that cordite emits no more than a blue haze when fired makes it score over gunpowder, the smoke from which can obscure a gunner's view – or give away the position of a sniper.

Verdun horsechestnut in bloom

A more positive use of the horsechestnut fruits is as soap. When mixed with cold soft water, the saponins found within conkers make a lather which is an effective soap. Try it with the leaves, which also have saponins: get someone to pour a little water over a horsechestnut leaf in your hands and rub vigorously until a slippery lather develops that leaves your hands soft and clean.

Soapwort is even richer in saponins and is used in the cleaning of the Bayeaux Tapestry.

A golden ash(10) for justice

It was Penny Jones of Amnesty International St Albans Group who suggested planting a tree to commemorate 'The Year of the Prisoner of Conscience' in 1977(11). She asked Paul Arnold to advise on a suitable tree and he chose an ash tree because of the Saxon tradition that justice should be dispensed under an ash tree.

Paul went with Penny Jones to Ayletts Nursery to make sure that the tree was a good one. They chose a fine specimen of a golden ash, *Faxinus transioni*. The Parks Department dug the hole for the tree and supervised its planting in the top corner of Vintry Gardens, the corner diagonally opposite the Abbey.

Amnesty International head office supported the scheme and suggested that Mukhtar Rana, who had been a prisoner of conscience for 20 years in Pakistan, should be involved in planting the tree and speaking on behalf of prisoners of conscience and the way in which Amnesty International had helped in keeping his plight from being forgotten.

The tree was planted in a formal ceremony and Mukhtar Rana, a charismatic speaker, did the occasion justice. After his release, Mukhtar Rana was chairman of Peace and Human Rights Trust International and campaigned tirelessly and effectively for human rights.

Female ash flowers

Ash leaf buds are one of the few I can recognise in winter. They are right at the tip of the twig and as black as nature can get them and as steeply conical as an ancient Assyrian's pointed iron helmet. Beneath and on either side of

Olive flower

the leaf bud are found the smaller but also sooty and conical flower buds. The flowers come out before the leaves – which makes the ash a 'precocious' tree. At first the flower buds swell into a tight tiny fist of purple balls and then these elongate on creamy green stalks, the male flowers opening yellow with slender anthers, the female flowers opening more widely into a filigree of purple and then pale green – a bit like cream-stalked, purple-headed broccoli florets.

The ash is sexually confused – or perhaps we should say the species is 'sexually all-encompassing': some trees have all male flowers, and some have all female flowers, some have a single branch or two of one sex and all other branches of the other sex, some are male one year and female the next, and some trees have hermaphrodite flowers (each with both male and female parts). I like it that the botanical term for such hermaphrodite flowers is 'perfect'. The definition confirms what we all knew: humans are not perfect.

Fertilised flowers with female parts produce bunches of dry seeds known as 'keys', and these tend to hang on the tree right through winter, making the ash distinctive.

Our common name for the ash is the Saxon word for it: aesc, which also meant 'spear'. Its wood is pale, light and flexible making it ideal for tool handles, baseball bats, oars and, when steamed and bent, for bentwood furniture, umbrella handles and the like. The ash is a tree with practical uses.

Ash trees belong to the same family as olives, the Oleaceae, which is, to me, unexpected because their flowers and fruits, on which the taxonomy is usually based, seem so dissimilar. Can you see any similarity in the flowers? Or between ash keys and olives? But who are we to know: taxonomists have been working hard on the order Lamiales and they seem to have no doubt that the ash, olive, privet, forsythia, lilac and jasmine spring from a common ancestor, distinct from the ancestors of other families in the same order (Tudge, 2005).

I had difficulty in substantiating the tradition that the Saxons associated ash trees with justice. I searched the Saxon Chronicles (now online) to no avail. That was only negative information, however, not evidence that moots were or were not held under ash trees. I asked at the Museum of St Albans but was told that moots were held in important places, Maiden Castle, for example, but not, as far as they knew, particularly under ash trees. I was told that the Saxons did regard the ash as a significant tree: Edward the Confessor's Charter granting the Manor of Wheathamstead to Westminster Abbey defined its boundaries by the location of ash trees.

Paul Arnold's source for the tradition was 'Trees of the British Isles in history and legend' (Wilks, 1972). Wilks tells us that it was the gods in Teutonic legend who held court (was it even a court of justice?) under a mythical ash tree, the World Tree, Yggdrasil, that reached to heaven and had roots down to the 'infernal regions' with squirrels reporting what was going on amongst the gods to an eagle in the topmost branches.

An intriguing legend, but it is not an association worthy of Amnesty International's valiant fight for justice.

Opposite: The golden ash planted for justice

I was then told by Chris Saunders, who used to work at the Museum, that in our own St Albans, the Abbot held his manorial court under the Great Ash in the Abbey courtyard. He directed me to the Victoria History of Hertfordshire which is online, and there we can read that 'For the trial of all crimes, pleas, and plaints the townspeople had to go to the Hundred Court of the Abbot's Liberty, which was held before the steward of the liberty under the great ash tree in the courtyard of the abbey.' Equivalent courts were held under ash trees in Midhurst (in what is now West Sussex) and Swathling (now a suburb of Southampton).

Imperfect as the hundred courts were, at least we can be sure of the link between ash trees and earthly courts of would-be justice.

Holm oak for ecumenism

There was a surge of support for the ecumenical movement in the 1970s and Paul Arnold wanted to do what he could to support it. He had read in '*Trees of the British Isles in history and legend*' (Wilks 1972) that, for people in Tudor times, holm oaks symbolised the Papacy and that many were destroyed by Protestants in the purges of 1536 (ibid. p115). I can find no corroboration of Wilks' statements but no evidence found is not proof that it did not happen, and we have as near as we can get to a tree that represents Roman Catholicism. Paul thought it would be a good ecumenical gesture to plant the Catholic tree in the grounds of the Protestant cathedral: the tree could commemorate the only English pope, Nicholas Breakspear who became Pope Adrian IV.

The authorities at the cathedral accepted Paul Arnold's suggestion and the local Roman Catholic community was keen and an apostolic delegate was appointed to officially plant the tree.

The holm oak destined for the Abbey Orchard was in the Council nurseries in New Greens. It was a big tree and hard work to move. The team dug trenches on four sides of the tree and lowered a steel hawser into the trenches. They dug a trench from the trenches to a nearby telegraph pole and anchored the hawser to it. They then tightened the hawser until it sliced like cheese wire through the huge root ball of the tree. They encased the tree and its roots and surrounding earth in sacking, 'like a pudding cloth', and used a skip lorry(12) to transport it through the streets of St Albans before the crack of dawn, careful all the way to avoid telegraph wires. The skip lorry was a brilliant transporter because it was low slung and had the mechanism to swing the tree outwards.

A hole of appropriate enormous size was dug, not without difficulty. As they dug, the men came upon the top of a brick arch. A member of the Museum

staff had to be consulted and he suggested it was the top of a tunnel from the Abbey to the Sopwell nunnery. He was joking – there are always stories of underground tunnels from monasteries to nunneries, but I understand that they are not generally given credence and certainly not here. There are, however, tunnels from the Abbey towards George Street perhaps for ease of provisioning, and there are remarkably substantial underground drains that lead from the Abbey roof gutters down into Abbey Orchard. The drains are

The skip lorry
swung the holm
oak into position

big enough for men to crawl through and it was probably one of these that the
Parks people encountered.

Another hole was dug clear of the arch and the tree lowered into the hole,
the arms of the skip lorry swinging it out and down into the hole.

The men packed a good bit of soil round the tree but left some space
and more of the compost made from autumn leaf sweepings to finish the
job. They also left a small heap of carefully sifted compost for the official
'planting'. When it is a lady mayor doing the job, a spoonful of soil is put on
a dainty trowel, the trowel is held while photographs are taken and then the
trowel is tipped to let the soil trickle round the base of the tree while more
photographs are taken. However, the apostolic delegate was no lady mayor but
of the more robust Christian kind and knew how to shovel soil and plant a
tree properly. He polished off the sifted compost in one sweep and then dug
his shovel into the unsifted compost.

'We are going to get the last laugh,' said one of the Parks men. They had
not been included in the introductions to the apostolic delegate: the cathedral

Opposite: The
holm oak planted
for ecumenism

officers at the time had presented him to the civic dignitaries, the Lord High Sheriff of Hertfordshire and august churchmen, but not the Parks men. I can imagine how it was: the churchman would have had his head full of all sorts of responsibilities and names to remember and was distracted. However, the Parks people regarded the project as their own, and they were miffed.

The 'laugh' was that the composted leaves collected from pavements and park corners held all sorts of unexpected debris including condoms. It all floated into the air as the apostolic delegate shovelled the compost round the tree base. The latter, by the way, shook hands warmly with the Parks people when the planting was over.

There was a photograph of the planting in 'abbeynews' of 3 May 1974. The caption reads '... The apostolic delegate said at the ceremony ... that he hoped the ecumenical movement would deepen understanding between the Churches as the roots of the tree went deep into the soil, and that friendships between Churches would multiply like the leaves on its branches.' Our Abbey Orchard holm oak is densely leaved all year round and its roots must be deep in the soil to keep it growing so healthily. It is as if the tree is doing its part to encourage us to fulfil the apostolic delegate's plea for friendship between the churches.

To find the tree, walk down hill across the front of the west face of the cathedral, out through the railings into the Abbey Orchard and continue on the path ahead; you soon come to a four-way crossing of asphalt paths and the holm oak planted for ecumenism is right there.

The tree also commemorates Nicholas Breakspear whose family lived in Bedmond. His father, Robert, became a monk at St Albans Abbey. Accounts differ as to whether Nicholas was a pupil at the Abbey but he certainly was not accepted there as a monk. He went to France and became a lay brother, then ordained priest, prior and eventually abbot in the Augustinian monastery of St Rufus near Avignon. From there, he was called to Rome where he was consecrated Bishop of Albano, an area in the Alban hills south of Rome, and then created Cardinal.

In 1152, Eugenius III sent Cardinal Breakspear as Papal Legate to Scandinavia to help decide the organisation of the Church within Norway, Sweden and Denmark. It is perhaps significant that he was away for these two years. Sometimes, someone who has been away is not seen as belonging to the inevitable factions that develop within an institution, and is acceptable to all parties. This may have been the case, or it may have been that he was known for being 'prudent, scholarly and disciplined'. For whatever reasons, when Breakspear returned in 1154, he was elected pope and reigned as Adrian IV for four years.

It astonishes me that near-on a thousand years ago, a lad from Bedmond in Hertfordshire could establish himself in France and then Italy and travel to Scandinavia and back. I understand that he was moving within the institutions of the Church in which Latin was universally understood, and that latterly he had the protection and resources of the Church but, none the less, he covered thousands of miles across territories(13) of many different languages.

The holm oak, *Quercus ilex*, is also known as the holly oak: 'holm' is thought to be the Saxon word for holly. It is also widely known in Britain as the evergreen oak, despite not being the only oak that is evergreen: the cork oak (*Quercus suber*), live oak (*Quercus agrifolia*) and several others are, too.

Holm oak leaves are a glossy dark green on top and silvery beige and hairy underneath – and there are masses of them giving the tree a density throughout the year. The branches grow out and up so that the tree as a whole has a pleasing rounded shape.

Male catkins appear in early summer along with tiny pink-tipped female flowers. Acorns are smaller than those of the English oak, a vibrant green nestling deep in a plump grey textured cup.

On a guided walk round Kew gardens, we were told that oaks are particularly promiscuous trees leading to there being 300–600 species (depending who is counting) in the genus. To put this in context, there are only 10 species of chestnut and 10 species of beech, both genera being within the same family as the oak, the Fagaceae.

Hybridisation makes it hard for taxonomists to agree on where one species begins and another ends. There is also disagreement on which features reveal true evolutionary relationships, on which taxonomy aspires to be based. Holm oaks, in particular, do not fit comfortably into any of the genus-splitting now in progress (Tudge, 2005). Watch this space.

Stone pine for an ancient goddess

Visiting Verulamium Museum, Paul Arnold noticed on display a votive bowl filled with pine nuts because pine nuts, seeds of the stone pine, *Pinus pinea*, were found in excavations of the triangular temple in Roman Verulamium. Paul thought, 'That's our next historical tree planting'.

Paul Arnold knew from '*Trees and Shrubs Hardy in the British Isles*' (Bean 1970) that *Pinus pinea* 'has always been valued in Italy for its edible seeds and, as their husks have been found in the refuse heaps of Roman encampments in Britain, they appear to have been sent over for the use of the army in occupation'.

On hearing of this, I inferred, with my 21st century layman's understanding of offerings, that even a staple food such as was issued to soldiers would be an appropriate offering if presented in the right spirit to a god or goddess. However, Rosalind Niblett sheds a very different light on the *Pinus pinea* seeds:

> The suggestion that the temple was dedicated to Cybele is based on the discovery in what must have been votive pits in the temple court, of burnt seeds and scales from pine cones of the Italian pine (*Pinus pinea*). The pine figured in the rituals associated with the worship of Cybele and her consort Attis but the Italian pine is not a species that grows naturally in Britain, either the cones or a tree itself must have been imported.
>
> Niblett, 2001

Cybele was a goddess of earth, mountains and caverns and was worshipped as a protector of fortified places and cities in general. As great protectoress of cities, it is appropriate that her temple would be seen straight ahead through a triumphal arch as people entered Verulamium through the Londinium Gate. The temple had an external altar at its blunt point facing Londinium Gate with a backdrop of the plastered walls of the temple, probably embellished with Purbeck marble, fragments of which were found in the 1930s excavation (Niblett, 2001).

The cult of Cybele and her consort Attis increased in popularity in Britain through to the 4th century. For more about the bizarre rituals associated with Cybele and her priests, not recommended to be read too soon after breakfast, you could Google 'Catterick Attis'. Closer to home, 'An inscription on a pot found in a grave at Dunstable, 10 miles along Watling Street, tells us that the jar was dedicated to the dead person by a man called Regillinus, on behalf of fellow worshippers of Cybele' (Niblett, 2000). There is an informative display in Verulamium Museum about the temple, Cybele and her acolytes, who were called *dendrophori*.

Opposite: The stone pines plante for Cybele

The grove of *Pinus pinea* that Paul and the Parks people planted is as close to the triangular temple in Verulamium Park as the archaeological authorities would allow. Looking up the hill from the children's playground to the hypocaust building we see a line of trees going away to the left of it. It is towards the end of this line of trees that the grove was planted.

From plans of Verulamium that show the features in the Park, we can work out that the triangular temple is 50 metres from the concrete path along the hedge line lower down the hill and 200 metres from Londinium Gate. From the grove, Londinium Gate can be located by the red dog-poo box(14) in front of its railings. A football pitch is about 90 metres long and there are usually a couple of pitches marked out and their goal posts clearly visible between the grove and Londinium Gate so that we can think 'two football pitches from the Gate and half a football pitch from the hedge'.

Not all the trees planted in the grove survived. Another name for the stone pine is 'umbrella pine' and this makes it easy for us to tell which are the original trees: they are distinctly rounded on top. When Paul Arnold saw that replacements were of different species of pine, he realised that the people now responsible for trees in St Albans do not know of the historical connections. It was Paul telling me this that made me determined that the stories behind the trees should not be quite lost.

American trees for Rotary beginnings

People in the Rotary Club of St Albans approached Paul Arnold with their idea to plant a circle of American trees to commemorate the anniversary of the founding of Rotary International in America. Paul advised on the species to be planted and Rotary sourced and supervised the planting in the top corner of Westminster Lodge parkland between the athletics track and Verulamium Park.

There is an English oak in the centre of the circle and, on a plinth topped by a circle of wood, is a silver plaque with the Rotary emblem flanked by the dates 1905 and 1980. It reads:

> The trees surrounding this English oak which are all of American origin were presented by the Rotary Club of St Albans Verulamium in the City of St Albans to commemorate the 75th anniversary of the founding of Rotary International in Chicago U.S.A. on 23rd February 1905.

The planned trees in the circle were American, but life is not always easy and we have long ago lost a pin oak, a red oak, a balm of Gilead, an Indian bean tree, a cotton wood and a white ash.

Opposite: The silver maple in the circle of American trees planted for Rotary beginnings

The trees we have now(15) are interesting enough. If we take the plaque as the clock centre and 12 o'clock at the top of the hill, the trees are as follows:

At 6 o'clock, lowest down the hill, is a **silver maple**, *Acer saccharium*, not to be confused with *Acer saccharum*, the sugar maple. It is the tree that we first see as we approach the circle from below, a large tree with branches arching upwards. It is a native of eastern North America. It has an obviously maple leaf, although particularly deeply incised and fluttering to show the paler underside from which it gets its common name. The flowers start to come out while the pointed leaf buds are still tight closed: the silver maple, like the ash, is precocious.

Silver maple leaves

At 4 o'clock is a **box elder** or ash-leafed maple, *Acer negundo*, which has a most un-maple-like leaf. Most of the leaves are pinnate with 3, 5 or 7 leaflets but some of the leaflets are fused into a more maple-like three-lobed form: it is hard to believe they are leaves on the same tree. The flowers, too, are un-maple-like. Our tree is male and what we see in spring are clusters of long drooping

Box elder leaves

coral-coloured stamens. One of the distinguishing characteristics of the box elder is its smooth bright-green shoots, and it has an exciting twist to its bark. The box elder is distributed across eastern North America from Florida to Ontario. It came over here first in 1688 to the gardens of Bishop Henry Compton at Fulham Palace.

Box elder bark

Cockspur thorn leaves and flowers in spring

At 3 o'clock and 9 o'clock are **cockspur thorn**, *Crataegus crus-galli*, native to eastern North America. Although of the same genus, the leaves look nothing like the leaves of our own native hawthorns, either in shape or texture. The flowers are white and prettily clustered in amongst the glossy bright green leaves

which turn wonderful colours in autumn: purple browns and yellows, startling alongside brilliant crimson fruits. All cockspur thorn trees seem to grow at an angle like the ones in the circle.

Cockspur thorn leaves and flowers in autumn

Norway maple leaves

At 2 o'clock is a **Norway maple**, *Acer platanoides*, which is a native of Norway(16) and not on the original plan but an attractive tree whose deep red petioles and purple-green foliage adds contrast during the summer.

At 12 o'clock on the outer circle and 9 o'clock on the inner circle are two substantial **American limes**, *Tilia americana*, the leaves of which are distinctively as dark a green above as below and as large as my large hand. I am told by woodworking friends that when they order lime wood from America they have to call it 'basswood'(17). One of the uses of the wood is in making solid-body electric guitars and basses,

which is presumably where it gets its name. The shoots and buds are bright red so that in winter there is a confusion of long brown and red strands on both trees. They contrast with the bright green of the box elder on the other side of the circle. Winter can be a good time to enjoy trees.

American lime leaf

At 10 o'clock we have a **honey locust**, *Gleditsia triacanthos*. Our tree is the variety *inermis* which is without spines. It is an open floaty tree with fresh spring-green leaves that grow in an attractive swirl from the twig. Each leaf has tiny leaflets with no terminal leaflet giving the leaf as a whole an unusual rectangular look. See the write-up on the French Connection above for a note on why 'locust'.

Honey locust leaves and fruit

American mountain ash leaves and flower

Closer into the circle and between 6 and 7 o'clock was an American mountain ash, *Sorbus americana*. Shortly before I was due to lead people on my first tree trail for the Heritage Open Weekend, David Curry helped me with some last minute confirmation of tree identification in the American circle. Imagine my surprise when a week or so later I turned to point out the mountain ash only to see a fresh stump. I was told that it was seen to be a rather feeble-looking specimen and cleared away, but it may well not have been felled if people had been aware of its significance.

And, finally, we come back to the English oak, *Quercus robur*, in the centre of the circle. The word order on the plaque makes is look as if English oaks are all of American origin. Oaks are so closely associated with British identity that I had thought of them as originating in Europe, but evolutionary studies lead us to believe that they originated in South East Asia around 60 million years ago, which is about 20 million years before India rammed into the continent. Quite recent. The Eocene period was a warm time and the oaks were soon (within 5 million years!) found in China, Europe and North America (Tudge, 2005).

Martin Shuttlewood said that the trees in the American circle are his favourites and when I asked him why he said he liked it that someone thought of doing it.

That appeals to me, too. Good one, Rotary.

Roma Mills' robinia: a tree for radical thinkers

When asked to advise on a tree to honour Roma Mills' term of office as mayor, the first of the new millennium, Paul Arnold chose a *Robinia pseudoacacia*. This time it was not for the tree's French connection but its connection with William Cobbett, 1763 to 1835, the politician, radical and social reformer. It was made clear in the speech to mark the occasion that Cllr Mills was regarded as being radical and social reforming – which is quite an accolade.

The tree is close to the wall round the tennis courts at Batchwood. Is it leaning to the left?

The robinia planted for Roma Mills

A London plane for a Westminster horologist

To mark the anniversary of the death of Lord Grimthorpe, Paul Arnold thought it would be good to plant a London plane. This is because Lord Grimthorpe designed the workings of the Westminster clock that we all call Big Ben (the name ought, technically, to be reserved for the big bell in the clock). As a millennium project, a replica of the clock was renewed. It is in the turret at the side of Batchwood Hall which Grimthorpe built and lived in. Grimthorpe's London plane is still not much more than a sapling. It is the small tree right in the centre of the photograph of trees and roses in front of Batchwood Hall. It is bright green against the darker trees behind it and on either side. The sapling destined to be planted broke a limb and another one had to be planted in its stead. You will be pleased to know that a splint has saved the spurned sapling and it has thrived, planted in the woodland close by in Batchwood.

The plane sapling in the centre of the photograph was planted to commemorate Lord Grimthorpe

Alder buckthorn for a battle with firearms

One of Paul Arnold's historical connections that particularly appeals to me is that between Bernards Heath and the alder buckthorn, *Frangula alnus*. The charcoal of the alder buckthorn can be ground to a particularly fine powder and was plugged down into the barrels(18) of hand guns with saltpetre and sulphur to make gunpowder. Hand guns were 'used, probably for the first time in a pitched battle on English soil, at the Second Battle of St Albans' (Burley *et al*, 2007) – which is quite something to commemorate and Paul Arnold did so by planting a grove of alder buckthorn on Bernards Heath.

A great part of the Second Battle of St Albans was fought across what is now Sandridge Road and Bernards Heath. The firearms were worse than useless in the battle: the men were busily fighting before they could load the cumbersome things. They are described as minature cannons held against the chest or under the arm, which sounds more dangerous to the gunner than the enemy.

I cannot find any alder buckthorn on the Heath and would be glad to hear from anyone who knows exactly where it was planted and if the trees have survived. Or go on a hunt for a small bushy tree with no thorns, rounded leaves with a pointed end, small, white, star-shaped flowers that appear in clusters in June, and small round berries that ripen from green to scarlet. It is the food plant of the brimstone butterfly.

A walnut tree for Nathaniel Cotton

Paul Arnold knew that Nathaniel Cotton, an early psychiatrist, had lived and worked in St Albans, and wanted to plant a tree to commemorate him. Nathaniel Cotton and his wife are buried together in St Peters churchyard so that seemed the right place for the tree, and Paul thought of the shape of each half of a walnut kernel and how like a brain it looks and decided a walnut tree would be appropriate.

Nathaniel Cotton is particularly remembered in St Albans for having founded an asylum which he called the *Collegium Insanorum*. It was in Lower Dagnall Street across the top of Spicer Street and, when part of the asylum was demolished to create a link to the new Verulam Road, the link road was called College Street. From maps showing the College when it was entire, we see that it was a substantial U-shaped building with extensive gardens and properly laid-out planting.

Cotton's most famous patient was William Cowper the poet, who suffered extreme depression and came to Cotton in December 1763, leaving in 1765, much restored. Cotton was a forward-thinking practitioner and encouraged his patients to talk through their problems. He also encouraged them to walk, and it is said that Cowper was to be seen walk, walk, walking the streets of St Albans, carrying a lantern if it was after dark.

In the collections of the Linnaean Society of London is a letter from Nathaniel Cotton to Richard Pulteney(19) offering to care for a patient for three guineas a week, adding that some patients paid five guineas weekly. Using the retail price index tables, this equates roughly to what we would expect to pay today for residential care of someone with, say, mild dementia. If we use average wage tables, however, we find that the terms would have been unaffordable for a wage earner in the mid-18th century. No doubt Nathaniel Cotton did charitable work – he was a devout Christian active in the non-conformist church – but it would have been mainly the gentry that he catered for.

Cotton's gravestone is the centre one of three lying flat to the earth south east of St Peters church. We can only just make out the words cut into the stone: 'Here are deposited the remains of Ann Hannah and Nathaniel Cotton'. Cotton and Ann (née Pembroke) had eight children and, after Ann died in 1749, Cotton married Harriet Everett in 1751 and they had three children.

Nathaniel Cotton's gravestone is the centre one of three

The walnut tree planted for Nathaniel Cotton is in the low-walled garden to the east of St Peters church. This is the Garden of Hope. It used to be a garden for the blind with a handrail round the edge, and there were sweet smelling plants and benches. The benches have gone but, where they used to be, are recesses in the surrounding low wall. Take the path left into the Garden and then the path across the grass behind the grey stone sculpture, 'God is with us'. Beyond the recess ahead is a four-stemmed tall tree with a pale-beige rough bark and floppy pinnate leaves. This is the walnut tree planted for Nathaniel Cotton.

The tree is said to be easily confused with an ash: the leaves are pinnate like the ash but larger and glossier.

Left: Walnut leaves

Opposite: The walnut planted for Nathaniel Cotton

Walnut catkins appear in spring and are huge, green at first then turning dark yellow.

The scientific name for our walnut tree is *Juglans regia*. All Juglandaceae produce – in their bark, their leaves, their husks and their roots – chemicals called 'juglones' that are noxious to other trees. This benefits the walnut because it hates the shade and needs to be the dominant tree in a group to survive (Tudge, 2005). The 'regia' means royal.

Nathaniel Cotton's walnut tree in St Peters churchyard is at the opposite end of St Peters Street to the robinia that started Paul Arnold planting trees for their historical connections.

From the tree planted to commemorate a temple that in some form existed before the Roman occupation to a tree planted for a mayor at the beginning of the third millennium, Paul Arnold's trees represent two millennia of St Albans history.

Walnut catkins

WILLIAM COWPER ESQ.

William Cowper, Nathaniel Cotton's most famous patient, © St Albans Museums

Paul Arnold's trees revisited

(1) I am sad to say that Paul Arnold died in 2014. I am glad that he knew that his extraordinary contribution to the community was appreciated.

(2) The robinia at the end of French Row was in obvious poor health in 2017 and felled in August 2018. See 'Fallen Trees'.

A tree in this position is a 'highway tree' and therefore the responsibility of Hertfordshire County Council. County Councillor Chris White is negotiating with officers to have it replaced with a robinia to keep the 'French connection'. We hope, also, that work will be done to reduce compaction and increase water and nutrients available to our tree's successor.

'Highway trees' include trees growing on minor suburban roads – even those growing between pavement slabs. St Albans District Council is responsible for trees on land it owns: mainly parks, open spaces and Council housing land.

The white on black board outside the Fleur de Lys in French Row

(3) In case the white-on-black board on the wall of the Fleur de Lys is ever removed, here is a photograph of it.

I cannot fathom what the two dots and then the 3 dots signify. Something omitted from a text? The County Museum became the Museum of St Albans and then, in 2018, was demolished except for its façade, and its contents moved to the St Albans Museum + Gallery in the Old Town Hall, Market Place, St Peters Street.

(4) There is yet another possible connection to the 'French' of French Row. It goes back to 1068 and the Doomsday Book. The 'Doomsday online' St Albans entry quotes 'Households: 16 villagers. 13 smallholders. 12 cottagers. 4 Frenchmen. 46 burgesses' and explains that the listings are households rather than individuals. I wonder what brought the Frenchmen to St Albans and whether there were Frenchwomen as well as Frenchmen in the households.

(5) Thanks to St Albans Civic Society and St Albans District Council, our tree that commemorates the Battle of Verdun now has a graphic information board designed by Roy Bellamy. It offers an evocative contemporary photograph of the Battle site and an account, in French and German as well as English, of the Battle and the story of our tree that commemorates it.

On Armistice Day 2016, a moving ceremony to commemorate the centenary of the Battle of Verdun took place at the Verdun tree.

A photograph was taken by Danny Loo on behalf of the Herts Advertiser from the same view as the original taken in 1976.

The 100-year commemoration of the Battle of Verdun, Armistice Day 2016

Our Verdun tree was put forward as one of the trees that people could vote to be England's 'Tree of the Year 2018'. It is too early to know the results of the vote and whether it could be selected to represent the UK in the 'European Tree of the Year 2018' competition.

(6) When I heard that there were Verdun horsechestnut trees in Windsor Great Park, I wondered whether perhaps our tree had been grown from second generation descendants. It matters not. It is the connection and our respectful commemoration that is important.

On the Internet, we can find a scholarly and comprehensive blog on trees grown from conkers and acorns brought from Verdun to Britain. Search for Nicky Hughes, Historic England, Verdun.

(7) The 'Old Contemptible' who planted our Verdun tree in Waxhouse Gate was Gordon Fisher aged 87.

I am grateful to Val Argue for unearthing the following extract from a local paper of the time:

> 'A very special tree is to be planted at the weekend to commemorate one of the bloodiest battles of the first world war.
>
> 'Old Contemptible 87 year old Mr Gordon Fisher of 115 Sandridge Road St Albans will plant the tree in the Waxhouse Gate Gardens on Sunday assisted by the Mayor of St Albans Eric Hewitt.
>
> *Herts Ad*, Friday 16 January 1976, p.4

(8) A fascinating fact is that the patch of colour on horsechestnut flowers is yellow at first, changing through orange to bright pink when the nectar has been taken from that individual flower, an 'out of stock' label as advantageous to the tree in promoting efficient pollinating as it is to the nectar-seeking pollinator (Thomas 2014).

Do have a close look at horsechestnut flowers. They look like white candles from afar, but they are beautiful and varied. It is said that flowers at the base of the panicle are female and fertile, those in the middle hermaphrodite and those at the top, male. This ties in with the fact that conkers develop only at the base of the panicle, and never more than 5 of them per panicle. I don't know why the hermaphrodite flowers are not fertile, and I don't know why all the flowers seem to me to have stamens and swollen anthers. With the naked eye, we can see the stamens as curved as ski-jumps, and even the colour and poise of the anthers which changes with the ripeness of its pollen. With a magnifying glass, we

Horsechestnut flower

can see the crimson tips at either end of the anthers, and the three intensely red spots on the stigmas. A delight!

(9) Alas, leaf miner grubs now obscure the wonderful colours of horsechestnut leaves we used to see in Autumn.

(10) St Albans District Council is committed to replacing trees of community value, and immediately offered to replace the Amnesty ash after it was felled in 2016 as part of routine tree management work.

St Albans Amnesty International chose a strawberry tree, Arbutus unedo.

It is only just a native tree: it is found in the west of Ireland. On the other hand, it is a particularly attractive tree: it is evergreen, has glossy leaves, bright red fruits, and delightful, bell-shaped, lightly fragrant white flowers.

Green fruits that will ripened on the Amnesty Strawberry Tree in Vintry Gardens

You might be reassured to know that, because of the Vintry Gardens historic status, an archaeologist was present when the hole for the new tree was dug in case some article of antiquity was unearthed. Nothing appeared.

The new tree was planted on 21 May 2018 in a moving and informative ceremony.

The presence of Mukhtar Rana's family, their words and the words of the Mayor made the ceremony moving. The few words individual Amnesty leaders shared about their work to support people made the ceremony informative.

Mukhtar Rana's grandchildren and Mayor Cllr Iqbar Zia assisted at the planting of the Amnesty Tree

(11) Two corrections: The Year of Prisoners of Conscience was 1977, not 1976. The original ash was likely to have been a *Fraxinus excelsior* 'Aurea'.

(12) It has been pointed out to me that the holm oak in the photograph on page 15 is not arriving on a skip lorry but on a low trailer. The skip lorry was used, not as a transporter, but a crane to lift the tree from the low trailer and then to swing it into position over the hole, as seen in the photograph on page 16.

(13) I have been told that Cardinal Breakspear would have travelled to Scandinavia from Italy by sea, not land as I envisaged. I still think it must have been an amazing journey.

(14) Most of the railings around Londinium Gate have been taken down but you will be happy to know that the red dog-poo box is still there so that you can line it up with the site of the Roman triangular temple.

(15) You and I could be the only people who know that a clump of trees between the athletics track and Londinium Gate was planted as a circle of American trees. The plaque telling why it was planted was replaced but has again disappeared.

The plaque that was at the centre of the circle of American trees

The trees themselves have grown into and over each other but, except for one of the cockspur thorns, they survive, and are identifiable from the text on pages 24–26. Perhaps the surviving cockspur thorn could be said to be at 8 o'clock from the central English oak. Perhaps there is no need to refer to an outer circle: the limes are easily identifiable as being at the top of the clock, 12 o'clock and 10 o'clock, say. Perhaps the honey locust could better be described as being 'level with the 10 o'clock lime, nearer the running-track hedge'.

Perhaps, too, because it is so close to the Circle, we should mention the attractive conifer at the corner of the running-track hedge, immediately down hill from the honey locust. Its foliage is an attractive deep blue-green and upward curling in an optimistic way. The leaves are cords of scales, not needles, and I have no idea of its genus, let alone its species.

(16) The northern-most extent of the distribution of the Norway maple is the extreme southern tip of Norway. Goodness knows why it is called a 'Norway' maple.

(17) Lime bark yields raffia-like strands that used to be used for garden ties and other tying or binding jobs. The lime strands were known as ' lime bast' or 'basswood', and this is much more likely to be the origin of the designation 'basswood' than the wood's use for guitar making.

(18) At the Second Battle of St Albans, charcoal, saltpetre and sulphur might well have been 'plugged down the barrels of hand guns' as I described, but that is not the way to make gunpowder. It is made at a factory or mill, the ingredients are combined damp so that they do not spontaneously ignite, and the resultant gunpowder ('black powder') is granular. The grains of properly

made gun powder ignite progressively, accelerating the ball or bullet along the barrel.

If gunpowder is a loose mixture of ingredients, it is likely to explode entirely at the base of the barrel, blowing up the gunner.

I hope you did not read the 2010 edition and use my description to make your own gunpowder!

(19) Like Nathaniel Cotton, Dr Richard Pulteney FRS FRSE FLS was a non-conformist and physician. He was also a botanist, wrote a biography of Carl Linneaus and promoted taxonomy. Although mentioned here only in passing (as sending a patient to Cotton), it is interesting that Pulteney should have a connection to both Nathaniel Cotton and to trees.

oney locust
the American
ircle of trees

Trees with history

Many more trees than those covered in the previous chapter have associations with past and present people linked to St Albans District. This chapter tells of some of them, and also highlights some old trees which in themselves represent history.

Two cedars of Lebanon(1) for Spencer ladies

Our most favourite tree, the cedar of Lebanon in Sumpter Yard, was planted by the Dowager Countess Spencer on 25 March 1803 (Toms, 1962). On the other side of the Abbey is another cedar and it was planted by the Dowager Countess Spencer's great great great great granddaughter, Princess Diana, when she came to the dedication of the rose window in the south transept. If we look upwards from Princess Diana's tree we can see the rose window.

In another 200 years, perhaps the great great great great granddaughter of Princess Diana will be Queen and come to plant a cedar on another corner of the Abbey.

Lady Spencers Grove

There is a thrilling passage lined with ancient lime trees and horsechestnuts leading from Grove Road on Holywell Hill through to the Abbey Orchard. It has its own street sign(2): Lady Spencers Grove. To be within it, is like being in a fan-vaulted cathedral: our eyes are taken upwards to the wonderful branching patterns of line and light, lifting us from the mundane.

The Lady Spencer is, again, the Dowager Countess who planted our most favourite tree, the cedar of Lebanon in Sumpter Yard. When her husband John, 1st Earl Spencer, died in 1783, the Dowager came to live in Holywell House which was in the middle of Holywell Hill and the road went round the house where Grove Road is today. The Dowager Countess lived there until she died in 1814 and it is said that she used to use this passage to get from home to the Abbey.

Opposite:
Cedar planted by
Princess Diana
in the Abbey
churchyard

Lady Spencers
Grove

The trees in the Grove are very old. I would like to think that young trees
will be planted between the existing ones, and the old ones removed as becomes
necessary. It may be difficult, however, because it would be shady for saplings.
It will be interesting to see what the experts in the Council decide to do.

Look out for a bullace plum along the Grove, by the way. It has pretty
blossom in spring and round red fruits in August.

Gombards yew trees

In 1998, it became apparent that the roots of the yew trees opposite The
Spotted Bull(3) in Verulam Road were pushing out the retaining wall, making
it unsafe. Initial rough estimates by the Council were that it would cost more

We might have
lost these yews
n Verulam Road

than three times as much to somehow rebuild the wall and retain the yews and a copper beech tree than to clear and level the site. St Albans people were upset and some of them met in The Spotted Bull and formed themselves into the 'Save the Gombards Yews Group'. The wall and the trees behind it were at the edge of the garden of Gombards House which was where the garages are now behind the trees. The passageway through the trees is known to local residents as Gombards Alley, hence the Group's name.

The Group collected 3,000 signatures to a petition, raised funds, put up posters, obtained extensive coverage in local newspapers and on local radio, and lobbied councillors. A civil engineer within the Group put forward an anchoring scheme using metal plates and steel rods which would save the trees and the wall more cheaply than the Council's first estimate. This scheme was the one adopted and the yews were saved for £14,000.

The participants in the campaign felt that 'a part of St Albans heritage had been preserved just because people were determined not to lose it'. Some of the funds raised went towards sponsoring a tree. See 'The Tree Sponsorship Scheme' in 'Trees and the future'.

A pagoda tree(4) in Abbey Mill Lane

As we walk down Abbey Mill Lane from the Abbey Gateway, we come to a pleasingly symmetrical white house on the right, Abbey House, which has been the residence of the Bishop of St Albans for many decades. Lord Runcie,

250-year-old
pagoda tree
behind Abbey
House in Abbey
Mill Lane

THE REMARKABLE TREES OF ST ALBANS REVISITED

who went on to become Archbishop of Canterbury, lived here from 1970 to 1979. In its garden is a veteran pagoda tree. We can see the tree above the wall and, if we peep round the gate a little further down the hill, can get a glimpse of its graceful spreading form and superbly weird trunk markings. Brian Lee logged it on the Chiltern's Special Tree Project(5) website, www.chilternsaonb.org. There we can see a photograph of the tree taken in 1884. It is an idyllic picture of 'Mr Hales the gardener and his wife and C.S. and J.P. Nisbett sitting down'. The branches of the tree curve upwards in a beautiful shape, a large tree in front of a substantial house and wide garden.

Brian Lee reports that the girth of the tree is 5.2 metres, its height 26 metres, and its age, though no documentary evidence has yet been found, is estimated to be more than 250 years. That takes us back to the mid 1700s when

St Albans was beginning to be an important staging post for carriage and horses.

James Gordon is credited with bringing the pagoda tree to Britain in 1753, and Brian Lee wonders if our tree could be one of James Gordon's original specimens. Brian also tells us that the tree has flowered recently – the pagoda tree has hanging inflorescences

Crusty bark of the pagoda tree

of creamy white flowers – and is in good shape, which is excellent news.

It was only yards away, in the Abbey Orchard, that another pagoda tree was planted. STAND, the anti-nuclear group, planted it to mark the first British Hiroshima Day in 1985, 40 years from the dropping of the nuclear bomb on the city of Hiroshima in Japan. This tree has not survived so the one in the Abbey Gate Offices gardens must serve to remind us of the day.

The scientific name for the pagoda tree is *Sophora japonica*. It would be appropriate if the genus name were derived from the Greek root meaning wisdom so that we would be reminded that with wisdom we can work out how to avoid war. However, it seems more likely that it comes from an Arabic word 'sophero' meaning butterfly-shaped – which has the positive connotations of beauty and regeneration. The tree belongs to the pea family – as does the robinia that I think it resembles – and the individual flowers could be seen, at a stretch, to be butterfly-shaped.

Despite the scientific species name, the tree originates in China not Japan, but it was often planted in the grounds of Buddhist temples in Japan giving rise to the common name, pagoda tree.

A tulip tree(6) planted by the Queen Mother

A tulip tree planted by the Queen Mother in the grounds of Wheathampstead School

Another tree to be found on a register of special trees is a tulip tree planted in the grounds of what was Wheathampstead Senior School in Butterfield Road, which runs east-west across the top of the hill linking the roads into the village from St Albans and Harpenden.

You can see from the photograph that it is a beautiful tree – and that, in July 2010 when the photograph was taken, it was in a construction site. In due course there will be housing here and the residents will be lucky to have the wonderful tree to enjoy.

A tulip tree for Elsie Toms

It was also a tulip tree that was planted for Dr Elsie Toms who wrote 'The Story of St Albans' and gathered old photographs of St Albans into a fascinating record of 'St Albans as it was'. She lived all her life in St Albans, was head of a secondary school in London and was first elected as a Labour councillor in 1945, was mayor 1960-61, was a councillor and alderman for 18 years, was a founder member of St Albans Civic Society, and worked to retain the character and beauty of St Albans and its surroundings.

The tulip tree was planted in the Abbey Orchard the year Elsie Toms died, 1982. She was 92 years old. Alas, the tree has completely disappeared.

A tulip tree for Jim Greening

A tulip tree was planted for the last mayor of St Albans City Council, Jim Greening.

Again it was a tulip tree that was planted for another mayor of the city, Jim Greening, the last mayor of the City of St Albans before it was expanded into the St Albans District Council. It is in the top car park outside the entrance to the Batchwood Golf and Tennis Centre. In early June the tulip tree has an unusual-looking flower and, in autumn, the whole tree is a pillar of molten gold ahead of us as we come up the drive into Batchwood.

The tulip tree has a distinctive leaf and flower

I have found that people of all parties speak well of Jim Greening. He and his family were friendly and hospitable. One of his missions was better facilities for the people of the City.

Old hedge lines

Here and there in our towns there is a line of mature oak trees, perhaps interspersed with the occasional ash, which tells us that this was once a hedge line, a field boundary. From aerial photographs we can see how recently there were fields being cultivated or grazed, for example on St Julians Farm. When St Julians housing estate was built, the field boundary must have been kept as a footpath/right of way because we can see a superb line of oaks running all the way from where Butterfield Lane comes through an arch under the Abbey Flyer railway line right up past Mandeville Primary School. There is a particularly majestic specimen in the open space by Holyrood Crescent. It has a girth of nearly 4 metres. Close to the playground, there is also a scrub oak that children clamber over. Who needs brightly coloured metal climbing frames! The real whopper of an oak, not quite on the line, is close to the end of Butterfield Lane in the gardens of Little Sopwell Cottage. One cannot but stand in awe.

On the other side of town, along the east end of Sandpit Lane there is another line of statuesque oak and ash trees and exceptionally fine field maples. Coming in from the east, perhaps from Welwyn Garden City or Jersey Farm, our eyes go to the stunning cedar at the top of the hill and we might not notice on the other side of the road the proud line of trees taking us all the way to the traffic light intersection with Marshalswick Lane and Beechwood Avenue.

Along the edge of London Road, too, there is a line of oaks and then of traditional hedging trees: hawthorn and field maple. And at right angles to London Road, at Kensington Close, there is a line of oaks.

It is interesting to look out for these lines of trees – we see them in Verulamium Park, too – and remember the use of the land, and the generations before us and their occupations in past times.

An oak for adventuring youngsters

A group of youngsters from Verulam and Beaumont Schools went wind surfing on the Mediterranean and were on their way to the Ardeche to do rock climbing and canoeing when their coach driver shockingly and tragically died at the wheel. Some pupils survived the resulting crash without injury, some were injured, many died. It was heartbreaking.

As one of the memorials to the youngsters, parents chose to plant an oak in the quiet of the walled Vintry Gardens in the lee of the Abbey church. As you enter Vintry Gardens from Waxhouse Gate, the oak is directly ahead,

An oak tree commemorates young people who were injured or lost their lives in a coach crash during a school adventure holiday

set in the grass a little further down nearer the Abbey. At its foot is a plaque telling the story.

The crash was at Ledignan in France on 29 May 1985. The tree was planted on 16 November of the same year.

A mountain ash for a pioneering lady journalist

At Batchwood in a spot where we can look out over the parkland of the golf course to views of the Abbey, a mountain ash was planted for Beryl

A mountain ash for Beryl Carrington

Carrington who worked on the *Herts Advertiser* for 60 years and was a life-long member of the Red Cross. There is a charming photograph and note about Beryl in James Corbett's 'A history of St Albans'. A mountain ash, or rowan, is a delightful tree with snowy blossom and bright red berries, a good metaphor for a spirited person and pioneering lady journalist. Beryl's tree had a lucky escape when a huge beech tree collapsed, taking with it half of an adjacent oak tree, but missing the rowan.

To find Beryl's tree(7), we go down the path beside the tower-topped stables alongside Batchwood Hall and then, when we are level with the ha-ha, turn left along the path through the trees. Soon on the right we see the damaged oak with a seat at its base and the beech logs beside it. Beryl's mountain ash is there at the edge of the parkland. Even though the marker with Beryl's name on it was chosen to be so discreet that it would not attract attention, it has disappeared. The great beech logs will be her pointer.

A cork oak for cross-cultural value

It was Donato Cinicolo who took me to see the cork oak planted by his respected friend George Pazzi-Axworthy.

If we go down London Road, pass the Highfield Park roundabout, pass the cemetery on the left, turn next right into Birklands Lane and then almost immediately right again (still in Birklands Lane), we see a right of way on the left. If we go down there, we find ourselves on a track that becomes a footpath. There is a lovely old white farmhouse on the right and, beyond it, a grove with a cork oak and a circle of stone pines.

A cork oak in Birklands Lane

The cork oak was planted by George Pazzi-Axworthy when he lived in the nearby old farmhouse. The Pazzi name is a very old and prominent one in Florence. George came to St Albans from Rome and married a Welsh lady. He grew to love Wales and its language and often visited with his family. As a lawyer, his advice was much relied upon by the Italian community among whom he was greatly respected. George's family went on many outings, collecting seedlings of various trees and taking them back to the family home, where they would be planted and lovingly tended. Trees were George's passion.

To me, this tree represents the value that different cultures and communities have added to our District over the years – the millennia.

An ancient yew in St Botolphs churchyard, Shenleybury

I am stretching a point by including St Botolphs because, strictly, it is outside the District – but only just, and we do not have another yew of quite this distinction. Its girth is more than 5 metres, 17 feet, making it between 600 and 750 years old (Robert Bevan-Jones in Miles, 2006). It would be neat to say that the tree would have felt the thump of Yorkist feet as the troops trudged to the Second Battle of St Albans in 1461, but they came up from Barnet along Watling Street a good few miles away.

St Botolphs church is now a private home but the churchyard is open to us. If you go south out of St Albans on Shenley Lane, the B5378, the churchyard is on the left behind a bus stop and opposite Shenleybury Cottages.

The ancient yew is the big tree on the right of the path towards the house. It is in good form: not a particularly tall tree and with a lovely rounded shape to its crown.

The canopy is dense and the trunk is wonderful with hollows and twists and curves and spaces right through it, the colours warm and varied. The branches elbow this way and then that: I could picture four men lying head to foot along some of them, which makes the branches about 24 feet long.

Looking up into the ancient yew tree in St Botolphs churchyard, Shenleybury

THE REMARKABLE TREES OF ST ALBANS REVISITED

The ancient yew has no fruit, it is a male[8] tree – a male coming into its prime with two or three thousand more years to go. As the millennia pass, the tree will employ strategies to keep it comfortable and regenerate its growth: it will push up new stems; lower its branches until they touch the soil, layer and regenerate; occasionally take a year off, or even a decade, and not grow at all (growth stasis adds to the problems of age estimation); and when its trunk is hollow it might drop some aerial roots down into the vacant space.

The church, now a home, is a fitting backdrop to our ancient tree. The flintwork is knapped (the surface smooth) and squared (each stone is made rectangular) and galleted (splinters of flint have been inserted in the mortar joints for strength). There are rows of larger stones and rows of smaller stones all tightly and neatly and beautifully fitted together.

Other venerable trees

Here and there throughout the district there are lovely old trees. There is the wonderful plane tree at the edge of Verulamium Park; the superb old beech in the Abbey churchyard; the magnificent poplar in the grounds of Kingsbury Mill; the pollarded limes in Romeland; an ash(9) in St Stephens field with a girth of 4 metres, exceptional for an ash; and in Rothamsted Park there are two oaks of 6 and 7 metres respectively.

Once we get our eye in, we find them – and can think about how long they have been there and the changes that have taken place around them.

Trees with history revisited

(1) The cedar planted by Princess Diana still does not look like a cedar of Lebanon by 2018. Perhaps in coming decades it will develop the plates of branching that distinguish cedars of Lebanon from other cedars.

(2) As at 2018, the street sign 'Lady Spencers Grove' is not visible. It has not been removed but is hidden beneath foliage. The Grove is alongside the Abbey CE VA Primary School.

(3) The Spotted Bull has since metamorphosed into The Brickyard and, as at mid-2018, is being converted into a dwelling.

(4) The pagoda tree in Abbey Mill Lane has had to be drastically pruned. I emailed a query about the tree to the Bishop of St Albans and his chaplain, Andy Crooks, replied, 'Bishop Alan has received your kind email and he has asked me to reply on his behalf.

'He is most grateful to you for your interest in the *Sophora japonica* tree.

'As you know, the tree has probably graced the garden here for well over two and a half centuries. Regrettably, in recent years there have been several instances of large boughs falling at random times.

Opposite: Ancient yew tree in St Botolphs churchyard, Shenleybury. It was 100 years old at the time Columbus sailed to America

'A professional arboreal assessment sadly revealed that the tree has heart rot and the reluctant decision was made to have it extensively reduced, both in order to make it safe and to extend its life.

'The tree is therefore not what it was, and it is no longer visible from the road outside. Andy added, 'I am sorry to have to convey the news about the tree's condition. Bishop Alan is both enthusiastic and expert in all things horticultural and it was a very sad and difficult decision to have the tree reduced.' It must have been. Andy said that for a good while, they could not use the garden for gatherings in case another branch fell. The Bishop is quite content for you to arrange for a photographer to visit, but you may want to reflect on this, given the tree in its present condition.'

We still thought it worth taking our own photograph of the tree.

We can no longer 'peep round the gate' to see the pagoda tree but here are photographs that show how severely it had to be pruned and how healthy it is looking now.

We are grateful to Barry Kimber for the photograph of the pruning work, and to Donato Cinicolo for the photographs taken in 2018.

The pagoda tree at Abbey House: cut back in Winter 2015, and flourishing healthily in 2018

THE REMARKABLE TREES OF ST ALBANS REVISITED

(5) The Chilterns Special Trees and Woods Project ran from 2006 to 2010, but the website still has an interactive map and, if you click on 'Special Trees and Woods' under 'Map categories', and then on 'Trees', the map becomes covered in little tree icons. Click again on 'Trees' to get rid of the icons so that you can see where St Albans is, then click on 'Trees' again and then on the icon at St Albans. Click on 'details' to get the whole story of the Pagoda Tree in Abbey Mill Lane.

Repeat the process to find lots of other special trees throughout the Chilterns.

The tulip tree planted by the Queen Mother in Butterfield Road, Wheathampstead, is now part of a woodland with maples and limes

(6) The tulip tree planted by HRH Queen Elizabeth the Queen Mother on 5 December 1967 in Butterfield Road, Wheathampstead, is thriving as at 2018.

It is now at the edge of a swathe of 25 (by my counting) maples of various species, making an attractive woodland between the houses and the road. Three young lime trees have been planted between the tulip tree and the entrance to the group of houses. All the trees are only 3 or 4 metres apart. They vie for the light but each seems to get sufficient sun to flourish.

(7) As at Autumn 2018, the mountain ash planted in memory of Beryl Carrington was covered in pretty berries and is thriving. It can still be found from the path described. See 'Batchwood revisited'. The damaged oak with its rustic seat is still there but not the beech logs that were a pointer to Beryl's tree.

A rustic seat marks the way to Beryl Carrington's rowan tree

(8) I state that the yew in St Botolphs churchyard is a male tree. Perhaps it will not always be so. The Fortingall Yew, a male, unexpectedly produced fruit in 2015. It is thought to be between 2000 and 3000 years old. Perhaps it knew of the local legend that Pontius Pilate was born under its shade and played beneath it as a child. Perhaps that cowed the tree into supressing its transgender propensities. Perhaps not until 2000 years later did the tree pick up the current zeitgeist and feel able to exhibit its female tendencies!

(9) The ash with a purported girth of 4 metres in the field below St Stephens church has succumbed to old age.

Our favourite trees

There was a good response to our call for people to say if they had a favourite tree or a tree that should be included in a book about St Albans trees.

We found that trees are important to people because of their age, their beauty, their rarity, their links to significant people or events – or because they have personal associations.

Some people had difficulty in limiting themselves to one tree:

Amanda Yorwerth's list

'Hope this isn't too late.

I have a few favourite trees in St Albans – take your pick:

1. **Lombardy poplars** on the south side of the little spur of Cell Barnes Lane that Nuffield Health Club is on. Although on private land, the trees are very tall and easily visible from the road. The best time to see, or perhaps hear, them is in the autumn when hundreds of starlings roost in them and they come alive with birds. When I cycle past them the sound of the thronging birds is a reminder that wildlife is here in St Albans and not just in far-off countryside or on nature programmes on the telly.

2. The spreading **prunus in Clarence park** between the cricket pitch and the park keepers' tool area. There is a bench near it. In mid spring the tree is like a great snow drift – absolutely beautiful. Even better, because the flowers are single, and so prolific the whole tree hums with insects – probably millions of them.

3. **Copper beech tree on the north side of Brampton Road**, near to the top of Blandford Road, in a front garden. An astonishingly big tree in a front garden, with fabulous, burnished, deep-burgundy leaves. How wonderful to see such a magnificent tree in such a suburban road and how lovely that some tree-loving person tolerates it whereas others would have found an excuse to lop or fell it.

Opposite: Pauline Barnes' favourite: a Wellingtonia in Highfield

4. Any of the **willows on the north banks of the Ver** near the road bridge next to the Nunnery ruins. Although the river authorities have hacked them about a bit to enable light to get to the river bed, if you look carefully you can trace the branches of these trees back to the main trunk and see the enormous horizontal reach of the branches – quite astonishing and, largely, ignored.

Amanda Yorwerth

The Handley-MacMath list

I am so sorry – my children and I took pictures of the trees we wanted to nominate, but after days of being too busy and the right people who can do digital pictures being too busy, I've given up and must just *tell* you which ones we wanted to celebrate, or it will be too late.

I'm afraid we wanted four – but we're a household of six – so I hope that's OK:

1. As you walk down Folly Lane and pause at the junction with Gombards, ahead in the distance is a field with one beautful, independent, **inconvenient tree** right in the middle of it. We never see it without a sigh of pleasure and relief.
2. We also love the tree – **the only(1) tree – you can see in Victoria Street**, which is mostly hideous and unshaded for commuters ploughing the whole length of it to the station and back. It's one of a group of beautiful mature trees on the corner of Victoria Street and Marlborough Road.
3. We're also very fond of the **trees in Gombards Alley** – the yews in the car park and the magnificent deep red tree near the steps down to the car park.
4. There's a **large tree in Knight's Orchard**. It is one of the few left to us since Chittendens have felled several – and is home to singing birds and a 'lung' to this part of the city. I look at it from my bed from dawn till 7am – again, with relief and great gratitude.

Paul, Tom, and Eleanor Handley
Trinity, George, Terence Handley-MacMath

Amanda Yorwerth and the Handley-MacMaths *were* too late for one of Donato Cinicolo's photographs but we can find their trees and see for ourselves what we think of their choices.

Other trees that people drew to our attention are sometimes included in another section: Paul Arnold's trees, for example. Where this is the case, I have quoted there the comments and mentioned the person who sent them in.

As was done for 'Favourite Trees' produced by Epping Forest District Council and for 'Plymouths Favourite Trees', we gathered a panel to judge which trees should be included in this book. It was decided that all the trees, together with the reasons for their selection, should be included and I hope that you will enjoy the trees and their stories as much as we have done.

A fantastic ash

The ash tree in the garden of a thatched cottage at 1 Lower Luton Road, Harpenden.

Fantastic 150 to 180-year-old ash tree clearly visible from the road.

Tom Thompson

When we went to take a photograph of the tree we found that it had been pruned recently and had nothing like the spreading canopy we can see from Google Earth that it used to have. It is shooting strongly, however, so we can look forward to it regaining its former extent(2).

Treasure Tots(3) favourite tree, an ash

Over the past six years, our tree has provided the Treasure Tots with

- shelter from the rain;
- shade from the sun;
- a place to climb up, sit in or jump down from;
- a safe place to learn by doing bark rubbings or looking for bugs;
- an interesting view when we hang things from its branches.

Our tree has allowed the children to have fun and it has provided/shared lots of laughter and tears with the children.

Our tree is the oldest member of Treasure Tots.

We hope you agree with us, that our tree is special.

> Parents of the children pictured here and Kim Parker-Mead,
> secretary to Treasure Tots Pre-School, Colney Heath

How could we not agree that this is a very special tree?

An aspen(4) tree

Mrs Meakin has chosen an aspen (a kind of poplar) in Heath Farm Lane.

> I can see the tree from indoors and outdoors. There is always movement in it and it makes a rustling sound. When I get up at night I can hear it and it sounds as if it is raining.
>
> Mrs Meakin

I like the idea of perpetual sound and motion. It is as if the tree is companionably seeking our attention.

Left: Rustling leaves sound like rain falling

Opposite: Treasure Tots Pre-School children under their favourite tree

The drinking tree

One curious characteristic of ancient walls is that they can provide the perfect environment for trees to prosper. So, if you go to Verulamium Park today, you can see portions of the great walls which are almost entirely covered in the woods of the park. One might imagine that some of the trees are the descendants of the seeds dropped by the guarding legionaries.

Only the walls were left behind after the predation of the stone gatherers. The walls were saved because their stones were set in a substance invented by the Romans but not seen in Britain again until the early 20th century: concrete.

Of course time has treated them harshly and what you can see today of the walls of Verulamium represent the product of both modern archaeology as well as the ancient skills of the original construction.

One particular tree has a mythical status for some of those who walk these walls today. Each morning the rain and dew collects in two pools cradled in the roots of the tallest tree in the park. Only in high summer do these secret pools dry up and every dog who walks the paths of the wood knows that there is almost always a cool drink to be found at the Drinking Tree. Legend has it that the spirits of the legionaries look over the animals that drink from these pools, protecting them from the dangers that the walls were built to resist. It is certainly true that there have been no hoards of arsonists from Essex since dogs started to use the tree. That can't be coincidence.

John Gilligan

The tree is on the Park side of the Roman wall not far from Londinium Gate. Once you have seen it, there is no doubt that you have the right tree because the roots have indeed formed a perfect bowl in which water collects. We accosted a dog owner asking if they would mind us taking a photograph of their dog drinking from nature's bowl of water and they and their dog knew all about 'the drinking tree' so John Gilligan and his dog are not the only ones who know about it.

A copper beech that holds the scene together

The copper beech located in the gardens behind the Gonnerston houses on Mount Pleasant must be one of the biggest trees in St Albans and can be seen from miles around but especially from Branch Road, Mount Pleasant and Kingsbury Avenue.

It is my favourite tree because it holds together several completely different periods of architecture by its dominant size and colour.

I can describe the periods of architecture that have a relationship with the copper beech as ranging from the white painted brick of the elegant Victorian Kingsbury Knoll to the uncompromising yellow concrete brick of the sixties Gonnerston. In between these periods

and sitting quite comfortably is the quaint part red brick, part chalk clunch(5) of Myrtle Cottage on the corner of Mount Pleasant, the red brick Edwardian houses of Kingsbury Avenue and the stark De Stijl style of the dairy building. Still within sight of the copper beech are the 14th and 17th century barns of Kingsbury Manor and the sober brick-and-tile 1920's Memorial Hall.

Where else can be found so many periods, styles and materials in such a small area as successfully co-habit the spaces around this giant copper beech?

Robert Merrick

These photographs that so well illustrate his observations are Rob Merrick's own.

Childwickbury copper beech for beauty and permanence

Rod Woodward proposed the copper beech in St Marys churchyard, Childwickbury Green:

> A fine well balanced specimen of a tree, clearly seen from the adjacent road or path; complements in colour the brick of the church building. Its presence provides a natural feeling of permanence to the church and surrounding houses, as the human population comes and goes over the years.
>
> Rod Woodward

Botanists refer to copper beech as 'purple', perhaps because it is only copper-coloured in Spring. Later the tops of the leaves do turn purple, but I cannot imagine we ordinary people changing from calling them copper beeches. I understand that landscape architects call such magnificent trees of strong colour 'accent trees'.

It amuses me that in the autumn the copper beech turns the same brown as all other beeches. It is as if it repents of its ostentation.

Leaves while they were still copper

A magnificent cedar and two giant sequoias

The cedar
between two
sequoia gigantica

Looking up into
one of the giant
sequoias

Just in case they have been missed. They were planted in the 1880s by Henry Bailey when he was building Cuckmans House, now demolished.

Brian Moody

I would have missed them – never dreamt they were there. As I drove to find them along the streets of Chiswell Green I still thought I must be in the wrong place but no, round a bend, there they were in Cuckmans Drive – these three amazingly dominant trees.

St Stephens cedar of Lebanon(6)

The tree has fantastic girth and height. I used to hang around it with my mates from St Julians (now Marlborough) School at lunchtime. One time my brother tried to climb it and got stuck and we had to call the fire brigade. It was really funny because he was about 35 years old at the time.

Jeff Smyth

We like this tree because it is so old and impressive and full of character. When we hugged it in 2008, the cedar tree measured 9m or seven adult hugs! There is also the rumour attached that Henry VIII courted Anne Boleyn under this tree!

Sandy Norman

It must be the oldest tree in Sopwell. We reckon it is about 500 years old at least.

Pam Smith

Left: Close in and looking up into the cedar

Opposite: The great cedar of Lebanon behind St Stephens churchyard

Cedars of Lebanon at Gorhambury(7)

I wrote to confirm some facts for this book and Lady Verulam added to her reply:

> Among our personal favourites here are the cedars of Lebanon which we think were planted around 1805. One fell down in the 1990 storm and we counted the rings.
>
> The cedars are visible from the permissive walk and, on house opening days, visitors walk right round them if they choose to look at the garden as well as the house.
>
> Lady Verulam

We see that one of the cedars has a tree house in it so presumably they are favourites for their joy as well as their beauty.

Cedar(8) at St Marys Redbourn

St Marys cedar is my favourite tree because of its lovely spreading branches and the cones underneath. With my friends, I used to collect the cones and paint them different colours and put them in a basket. I see this very old tree and think of the people who have passed under it over all the years gone by.

Stella King

Cedars for remembrance

Mrs Brenda Foster's favourite tree is the cedar of Lebanon on Hatfield Road in the cemetery.

I had not explored the cemetery before and found it neatly kept, peaceful and beautiful with well placed solemn tall conifers, spreading cedars, a lovely avenue of horsechestnuts, and also blossom trees that must be a picture in spring.

The cedar of Lebanon that Mrs Foster draws our attention to is near the entrance to the cemetery and close to the railings on Hatfield Road, so that we can see it well each time we pass.

Red and white for the Wars of the Roses

The alternating red and white cherry trees in Sandridge Road were planted to commemorate the Second Battle of St Albans during the Wars of the Roses. The Battle was fought here across Bernards Heath in 1461. White is for the House of York and red for the House of Lancaster.

Four people tell us that these are their favourite trees:

> They are such a feature of driving into St Albans in the spring. There is a mixture of the girly pink cherry blossom mixed with the darker red-leaved cherry trees with darker pink blossom, and now some new small trees which are a mottled pink, planted to take over from the older trees as they age. These are along the wide strips of grass at either side of the Sandridge Road, called the Wastes.
>
> Charlotte Thorp

> The trees cheer you up. It is spring after the long winter.
>
> Amad Purton

> The display in spring is spectacular and fine for the rest of the year – and it brings history and the dead to some form of life.
>
> Mel Hilbrown

> The blossom on any tree is uplifting but these especially so because of the interleaving of red and white and of old and younger trees – which makes it all last longer. In blossom time I make special journeys and detours to pass the trees and I think of the person whose idea it was, that they thought of us all and our pleasure on into years to come.
>
> Gill Curtis

Left: Not all the blossom comes out at the same time

Opposite: An avenue of red and white blossom for the Wars of the Roses. (I took this photograph: I did not find Donato Cinicolo until after the blossom had gone.)

I do not know whose idea it was to plant the trees, but it was done to celebrate George V's silver jubilee in 1935, which makes the original trees three quarters of a century old in 2010. The trees are steadily being replaced(9), again with ornamental cherries.

If we want to go native, would alternating red and white hawthorn give the same spectacular effect?

Clarence Park climbing tree

If you enter Clarence Park by the double gates nearest to the bandstand and playground, turn immediately left and walk just a few metres, you will come to our climbing tree. It is on your left opposite some rhododendron bushes.

The tree is an amazing shape with some great low branches for climbing and sitting on. I have spent many a time with each of my three boys when they were little watching them clamber about in this tree – far more entertaining than the playground!

Mary Liming

Sue Howard also refers us to a tree in Clarence Park that children love to climb. Sue says her tree is near the Lodge and she thinks, from memory, that it is a cedar. I think it is the same tree that Mary Liming tells us about.

The tree is a Lawson cypress. See how abundantly dripping down its foliage are its small spherical cones, blue in spring, yellow-green in summer and brown in autumn. After they burst to release their seeds, what is left of the cone hangs on in there. It is fun to take a magnifying glass to the spent cones and see their cubist angles. Male 'flowers' hang at the very ends of the floppy foliage. Tiny and black they fall off when they have released their pollen in early spring.

The Cumberland conifer(10)

The conifer in Cumberland Court lawn is my favourite tree because it is a fine example of a mature tree.

Despite buildings changing you can still picture this in the gardens of Borradale.

Note – Borradale is a surname from Cumberland, though John Borradale married Mary Arris on 8th June 1682, at St. Peters, in St Albans, where Mary's father, Thomas, was a doctor and local M.P.

Thomas Arris came from a family of eminent London physicians; his grandfather had been warden of the Company of Barber-Surgeons, and his father, Edward, was sergeant-surgeon to Charles I.

Edward founded the Arrisian anatomy lecture in 1645 and become Master of his company in 1651.

John and Mary Borradale's eldest child, John, was baptised at St. Peters on 13 May 1683, but it appears that the family had moved to Nottingham by 1693 (the date on the present plate) when his twin (?) daughters were baptised at St Nicholas, Nottingham, on 3 August of that year.

David Kaloczi

David Kaloczi tells us that the tree is in what was once the gardens of the large house called Borradale that stood where the Seventh Day Adventist Offices now stand on the corner of St Peters Street and Carlisle Avenue. Cumberland Court is a block of flats along Carlisle Avenue.

A fig tree is a living link with Italy

What precious thing would you take with you if you were emigrating?

When Donato Cinicolo's father came from Italy to St Albans in the 1950s he brought a cutting from a fig tree growing in his home town of San Bartolomeo in Galdo. Whenever the family moved within St Albans, a cutting from the original tree came too.

And now Donato and Rosie also have a 30-year-old fig tree in their garden where it flourishes and bears fruit. It provides a living link with Italy.

What an heirloom.

A venerable horsechestnut

The horsechestnut on the corner of Station Road and Harpenden
High Street is a fine old tree with widespread branches and deep
foliage. Every year it comes into bud a couple of weeks before all the
neighbouring trees and when it comes into leaf you know that spring
is really on the way. As Geoffrey says it seems to lift the heart. No
one seems to know why this tree is the first to flower. Some say that
its roots reach down to the stream which runs under Harpenden
Common at this point, others that it grows in what was once a
farmyard fertilised with centuries of manure, or that it is on the site of
an old abattoir! Whatever the truth it is a delight to see every year.

Maggie and Geoffrey Turner

The tree is braced by cables, which is just as well because children are often to
be seen clambering around its lower branches – and gown-ups after a few jars
seem unable to resist trying to climb up into it.

See how knobbly and interesting the bark is.

Chime Square horsechestnut

This tree is my favourite because it is a magnificent specimen of *Aesculus hippocastanum* (horsechestnut to you and me!) and must be about 80 foot high and is now [May 2010] festooned with beautiful white 'candles'. When I was a child I planted a 'conker' and was thrilled when it grew into a miniature chestnut tree. I now wonder what happened to it when we moved house. And to think that this specimen started in the same way – incredible!

From the Latin name I conjecture that Spanish castanets are made from horsechestnut wood. It can also be used to make toys, in cabinet-making, packing cases, and, in the old days, milk pails because of its whiteness. It is also sometimes used to make charcoal.

The name comes from the horseshoe-like marks to be found under the fat brown buds.

Pat Shea

This has to be the best example of a horsechestnut in springtime. It is a huge tree and the branches radiating out from the sturdy trunk have a wonderful display of 'candles' flowers. No doubt hundreds of conkers in the autumn. I do not know its age but it was always there when the bus garage was in use – before Chime Square was built!

Alison Chant

This tree is my favourite because of its great beauty, its size and all the changes it has seen over the years:

The beauty comes from the changes over seasons. In spring we have the fresh new leaves with the petalled flowers resembling 'candles' or small lupins. The large showy leaves of summer, leading to the 'fruit' which gives us our conkers. Winter shows us the bold shape of its strong structure.

The tree's size is such that people walk under it without appreciating its massiveness. It stands there, a symbol of power, defying anyone to try and move it.

This item could have been called 'Where have all the buses gone?' as our tree has seen so many changes over the years. At one time queues formed nearby as people waited in summer to board the 'special' buses to spend the day at Whipsnade Zoo. We had Green Line buses (712 Luton to Dorking; 713 Dunstable to Dorking) pulling in at

Opposite: Horsechestnut in the gardens of Chime Square on St Peters Street, the photograph taken in early morning light and before inevitable heavy traffic has built up

St Albans Bus Garage, as well as the L.T. bus No. 84 to Arnos Grove, which terminated here. Then we had our own Country buses: the 313 to Enfield, the 368, 369 to Dunstable whose home base was in the garage in the shadow of this wonderful horsechestnut.

So long may this beautiful tree stand tall and add glorious autumn colour for the pleasure of many generations of St Albans citizens to come.

Jim Mullany

... because it is so huge.

Anthony Nicholson

It raises my spirits. The tree looks magnificent in Spring when the 'candles' of flowers are in bloom.

There used to be another horsechestnut, even larger, which was shamefully allowed to be cut down by developers when the flats were built.

Cathleen Palmer

The Chime Square horsechestnut spreads above adjacent buildings. The tree was here in the time of our bus garage before Chime Square apartments were built.

St Stephens horsechestnut(11)

The magnificent horsechestnut located in the churchyard of St Stephens church adjacent to Watling Street, girth approximately 5.35 metres, height approximately 20 metres.

Reg Beer

We like this tree because it is so old and impressive and full of character and must have witnessed several historic occasions as well as hundreds of weddings.

Sandy Norman

It is so very old and a magnificent specimen of horsechestnut. No one is quite sure how old it is – but I think it is worthy of a mention in the book.

Mrs Nancy Walker

Geoff Dunk tells us that the horsechestnut tree in St Stephen's churchyard was planted on 22nd November 1785 (Dunk, 1985). We do not know the reason but we can picture the people who gathered round in knee breeches or wide skirts and powdered wigs. There has been great change since then.

See also 'St Albans churchyards' for a full-page photograph looking up into the tree.

A lone horsechestnut

I like the thought of hot hazy summer days sitting on the bench whiling away the hours. I like the thought that perhaps women in past times on an afternoon off could sit here too and relax. I imagine them on their own. I think it each time I pass.

Sarah Terry

The tree that inspires thoughts of peaceful solitude is on a path between The Swing Bridge pub on Southdown Road and the duck ponds on Harpenden Common.

An Indian bean tree on the Highfield tree trail

> I lead Health Walks around Highfield Park and this tree always causes the most interest and we have to tailor our walks to keep an eye on it throughout the seasons.
>
> Sue Hawkins

Below is a photograph of the leaves and last-year's beans on the tree in mid summer after flowering. The flowers are similar to the candles of a horsechestnut but larger and more open. In 2010, this tree finished its flowering earlier than the Indian bean tree by The Silver Cup in Harpenden and earlier than the one in Clarence Park. Try in early July for flowers but, as Sue Hawkins says, keep coming back at different seasons to enjoy the shape alone in winter, the great big floppy new leaves in late spring and the pendulous elongated beans throughout the year.

St Michaels Manor lime tree

The lime tree in the grounds of St Michaels Manor is my favourite tree because it changes with the seasons, is a home for birds, and is unashamedly large. I suspect that it is the tallest tree in St Albans.

Roger Sansom

You can see the tree as you walk up Fishpool Street. It is my favourite tree because, when I am walking home from the Six Bells at night and see the tree in the dark, the top branches look like two people kissing.

Well, they do to me!

Deborah-Jane Hilda Kishman

This tree was one of the 'Twelve Trees of Christmas' in 2003. It was 'dressed' by the Italian community of St Albans, and Guides and Brownies sang traditional songs. I wish I had been there.

The mistletoe lime in the Abbey Orchard

John Rae wrote me a letter that I treasure. Here is a reproduction of a sketch that he included:

Dear Kate, I told you about the tree beside (below) the Abbey where all the girls of St Albans stand beneath the mistletoe every Friday night.

John Rae

Oscar Wilde said 'I never, ever, exaggerate.'

A magnolia in the heart of St Albans

The magnolia tree in the little park behind St Peters Street, Hatfield Road
and the Council offices is my favourite because it is such a wonderful
sight when in bloom and so close to the busy centre of town.

Laurie Gibson

Magnolias are particularly spectacular because their flowers are out before
the leaves so that in April(12) we get the whole shape of the tree as a mass of
nothing but flowers.

It amazes me that magnolia trees are considered a possible candidate for
being the first of flowering plants to evolve: the first of angiosperms (Tudge,
2005). The flowers are so large and impressive that intuitively one feels that
they must have evolved well after those plants with less extravagant flowers.

Variegated maple

My favourite tree is a variegated maple down Waxhouse Alley, St
Albans, where the alley opens out to the north east of the Abbey and
the path curves round following the old vineyard wall. I love the old
flagstones, the old lampost, and the light shining straight through the
windows of the choir. But most of all I love the maple tree.

It is my favourite tree because of its beautiful shape and colour, and
the way it enhances one of the loveliest places I know. I love to see
this tree as I turn down Waxhouse Alley leaving the noise of the street
behind, or coming the other way up the slope from the Abbey. The
strong slim trunk and the perfect crown of leaves – a startling bright
lime green in spring, and a gorgeous deep crimson in autumn. Even
in winter I love its perfect form. I love its brilliant colours after rain
or early in the morning, at night by lamplight or on a stormy evening.
It is a picturesque spot already but the tree is the focal point of the
corner, bringing life and colour.

Andy Davies

....because it interestingly has two types of leaf. One is very bright
yellow/green, the other darker green. It is very good at the moment.

John Rae

A medlar

Nick Edmonds submitted as a favourite the medlar tree in his front garden in Cunningham Avenue, St Albans.

There is a medlar in Old Welwyn that has a plaque against it saying that it may be the only one in Hertfordshire so that it is good that we have one here.

The fruits look like tiny monkey skulls and are only edible once they are rotten. The tree originated in Persia and used to be popular in English Victorian gardens for its gothic effect: not only are the fruits skull-like but the trees look gnarled and ancient and interesting even in their early years.

Medlars are self pollinating and do not grow too large so perhaps they will become more popular again in today's smaller gardens. We would be well advised to learn what the Victorians knew: to wait until October to pick the fruit and then to leave it to 'blet' or until it 'reaches the bletting stage' – for which read 'has gone rotten'.

Monkey puzzles(13)

The monkey puzzle opposite the Sunrise Café in Southdown is my
favourite. Neighbours hang monkeys from the branches which makes
us laugh as we are sitting having a coffee in the café.

Robert Naylor-Stables

The fact that someone has hung monkeys on the branches is what appeals to
Elliot Tate, too.

Clare Raynor tells us that her favourite tree is the mature female monkey
puzzle in her garden at 37 Queens Crescent, Marshalswick. The tree is in the
garden behind the house but is just about visible from the street.

The monkey puzzle, *Araucaria araucana*, originated in Chile and Argentina.
The way the whorled shoots all curve upward gives the trees a confident jaunty
look which I find appealing.

Sander's Mexican lime

The tree in grounds of St Albans and St Stephens School, Camp
Road, behind No. 47 Camp Road and opposite Cecil Road, is
important to the history of this area. It was planted in about 1886 by
Frederick Sander, 'The Orchid King', whose orchid nurseries then
occupied this site. In recognition of Sander's links with the Royal
Botanical Gardens at Kew, he was presented with one of three such
trees in England. (The others are/were at Kew and Chorleywood
College.) This Mexican lime carries a 'TPO 42' protection. Its
winter skeletal form is beautiful and in summer its unspoiled form
impressive, culminating in an aromatic climax in August.

Tony Billings

The Mexican lime foliage is extraordinarily dense, pale underneath and
brighter green above.

The flowers are prolific and pendulous. Above each flower cluster is a
bract that looks like a slender leaf. It curls upwards and outwards adding to
the vivacity of the tree.

Copper beeches for Sander's sons

Tony Billings has given me permission to quote from his book 'The Camp':

> Today it is difficult to believe that Sander's orchid empire ever existed;
> all that remains is a group of trees which he planted.... Just below
> [the Mexican lime] is what appears to be a single lofty copper beech;
> actually it is a group of three trees Sander planted to mark the births
> of his sons Fritz, Fearnley and Louis.
>
> A sole red hawthorn marks the entrance to the Sander house.
>
> Billings, 2002

The red hawthorn has gone now. It went when a wicket gate into the school
grounds was inserted opposite Vanda Crescent a few years ago. But the
wonderful trio of copper beeches is here for us to admire.

An oak on the edge of Wheathampstead's oppidum

A majestic oak on the right hand side of Beech Hyde Lane as you go up the hill from Marford Road, Wheathampstead, is my favourite tree. It is around 400 or 500-years old and situated in the middle of what was a very big Celtic–Catuvellauni settlement marked on the map as 'Belgic Oppidum' (Belgic City).

The country lane sneaks around this special tree: a marker of time past, present and future in a landscape that has changed little in over 2,000 years. It also grows close to where the chieftain's palace was thought to be.

These are all reasons why this is my special tree. It is a tree of wisdom.

Neil Sankey

Beaumont(14) oaks

The tree in the rear garden of 63 Woodland Drive, St Albans, is my favourite tree. It is tall enough to be seen from the street (and of course from Google Earth!) and is probably the oldest tree still alive on the former Beaumonts Farm and already a mature tree when the original Beaumonts Manor was still standing in the 17th century.

I was born and brought up next door to the former Beaumonts Farm (near where the manor had been) at 57 Woodland Drive and the oak was part of my life as my bedroom was at the back of the house. Its enormous branches spread wide and almost over the roof of the nearest house. Today this would not be allowed and a park would be laid out around it, but before the war the developer/builder took no notice of such things and there were fewer regulations.

The tree was home to bats, red and then grey squirrels, owls, and a variety of other birds. The sound of leaves rustling in high winds was distinctive.

Some time after 1960 the tree surgeons were called in and spent the day clipping the main branches in an attempt to reduce the risk of damage to the house if a branch should fall. I still miss the form and life of the tree as it was before lopping.

Mike Neighbour

Vic and Vera Foster live next door to the tree, and its branches spread right across their garden. They say that the tree is like a metropolis with every kind of life within it.

At the other end and on the other side of Woodland Drive is a sibling oak(15) which is the favourite tree of Mary Robey in whose garden it stands guardian.

Left: The oak at 63 Woodland Driv▸

Opposite: The oa▸ at 6 Woodland Drive

A pair of oaks in a vicarage garden

My favourite trees are two aging oaks, both with TPOs, both showing their age. One is particularly notable(16) in its old age for hosting two other trees in its trunk: a laurel, and a rowan tree that is currently in flower and will bear berries in due course.

Mark Slater

The trees are in St Lukes vicarage garden, Cell Barnes Lane, St Albans, clearly visible from the side of the church.

One of the trees is a living miracle: a miracle because it is living. It has a decent canopy of leaves, especially considering its great age which is obvious from its girth, but it has only a ten-inch-wide strip of bark under which to get all the nutrients and water it needs to sustain that canopy.

Not only that: the tree has these other trees living off it. It was strange to see the rowan leaves amongst oak leaves on one side of the tree and laurel amongst the oak leaves on the other side. Each tree seemingly thriving.

Is our calm dignified tree showing us how little we need in order to be alive, that we should ask no more than to be alive, and that we can nurture whoever comes our way even if they are different from ourselves? How apt a metaphor for a vicarage garden.

Earlier pollarding has created a podium about 2.5 metres off the ground and Donato Cinicolo said, 'This tree needs somebody in it.'

'A vicar?' I suggested.

Mark Slater was up for it and went to put on a dog collar and get a ladder. Up he climbed and cheerfully posed for the photograph.

The second tree of the pair is equally venerable but has most of its bark intact so it looks more comfortable. I felt glad it is there to lend support to its companion. A fanciful thought, of course, because no doubt they are competing for nutrients.

I like the swing hanging between the two oaks: a sign of young things enjoying old things.

Oaks make a shady glade for a sunny Sunday morning

My favourite trees are the young oaks close to the Kohima Epitaph in Jersey Farm Woodland Park. The trees have recently become large enough to sit under on a hot day. We can look over the open fields and surrounding woodlands whilst keeping out of the sun.

The light breeze that the trees seem to produce beneath them even on a hot and still day is perfect for relaxing and appreciating the big skies and vibrant colours of the different trees and grasses.

Having an epitaph in such a beautiful position adds to the charm of the spot for me. When I look across the field or walk down to Sandridge I never fail to feel very lucky to be able to share this woodland and my favourite tree freely within the neighbourhood in which I live.

Anita Wall

The Hatching Green oak

As we go down Redbourn Lane from Harpenden towards Redbourn, the road curves gently left so that we see ahead of us a huge oak tree. It is on the corner of High Elms where the road begins to curve smoothly right.

> In its close juxtaposition with a lovely house in a residential environment this tree reminds us of the dignity and wonder of nature. May it endure, perhaps even outlasting the house.
>
> Ric Andrews

I do not know about the house, but the tree ought to outlast(17) you and me.

There is an altogether attractive sweep of trees here: first there are exceptionally tall ash trees above laurels and conifers, a weeping willow, the magnificent oak, a lovely spreading cherry tree, a balsam poplar and then another weeping willow. The leaves of the balsam poplar are aromatic.

St Albans Museum oak

A group of local residents, including historians, scientists and eminent politicians, were involved in the campaign for a museum in St Albans. It took fifty years to come to fruition but eventually the Hertfordshire County Museum (as it was then) opened in 1899.

Many objects were donated by local collectors. One of the most touching gifts of all was a sapling from the Great Oak at Panshangar House, Hertfordshire, which was donated by Earl Cowper. It was planted in the opening year and is now a mature oak tree.

I love this tree because it is so full of life and steeped in history. When I look at it I am reminded of the people who campaigned for the museum. I think of their pride and fascination with the history and archaeology of the area. I think of them in their straw boaters planting the little sapling, knowing, even hoping, that it would outlive them.

Elanor Cowland, Keeper of Community History
at Museum of St Albans

The Panshanger Great Oak was visited in 1789 by Gilbert White, author of 'The Natural History of Selbourne'. He lived in Selbourne in Hampshire so that it was something of a pilgrimage to come all the way to Hertfordshire. He commented favourably on the 'form' of the tree. I wonder whether then it had allowed its lower branches to rest on the ground. Certainly Jacob George Strutt tells us in his 'Portrait of Forest Trees', published in 1822, of the branches dipping down to the very ground (Morton, 2004).

The Great Oak(18) is still there but can only be visited by appointment with Lafarge Aggregates.

The gardens behind St Albans Museum(19), on the other hand, are open to us all and are a delight. They were laid out consciously to foster biodiversity. There is a pond and flowers and pathways – and our own Great Oak.

Nomansland climbing tree

It is known as 'the climbing tree' and some of the branches have been worn smooth by climber after climber climbing its branches.

Alex Laurie

I wondered if the climbing tree on Nomansland Common has been nominated? It's loved and smothered by small children all summer and looks amazing.

Sue Howard

When we went to take a photograph of the tree there were indeed children clambering over it. A father had brought his little ones over from Hatfield. He said that he has often met mums and dads who say that they used to climb on the tree when they were children and now bring their own family to enjoy it.

See how low the bottom branches of the tree are.

To find the tree from the Nomansland car park, cross Ferrers Lane and walk left under the trees to an open meadow. The ground slopes down and then up to a simple bench. Go down the slope and then to the right where you will see the climbing tree ahead.

London plane in Catherine Street

Ted Petts nominated the London plane tree in Catherine Street outside what we all call Bleak House but ought now to call Dalton House.

> About 35 years ago, I lopped and felled the beech tree that was there before because it was dead and dangerous. It was replaced by the plane tree and I have watched it grow over the years and love it.
>
> Ted Petts

How bleak that junction would be without Ted's lovely spreading plane tree.

Silver Cup plane trees

Belinda Naylor-Stables likes the trees beside The Silver Cup in Harpenden.

> These have beautiful prickly 'conkers' towards the end of summer.
> The leaves also turn wonderfully in the Autumn. The branches look
> fantastic against the sky.
>
> Belinda Naylor-Stables

It is usually horsechestnut fruits we call 'conkers', but plane fruits in their cases are equally spiny – and stay hanging on the tree like Christmas decorations.

Plane perfect

My favourite tree is the plane in Bricket Road, St Albans, at the side of the police station(20). It shows how important large trees are in the urban landscape.

Like others of its kind, it survives in about as hostile an environment for a tree as can be imagined: in the centre of a city, in a car park, surrounded by concrete with cars parked for the best part of each day as close to its trunk as they can get. Yet there it stands unpollarded, spreading its branches to obscure one of St Albans most unlovely buildings, helping to purify the air, providing shade and a home for wildlife, stately, beautiful, it lifts the spirits. It's a delight to the eye. Long may it remain!

Penny Jones

Penny's plane tree is not only at risk from pollution and compacting: it is one of a pair of planes and they, a copper beech, a silver birch and a liquidambar are all within a plot which is up for development(21).

Can we hope for an imaginative architect who could make the planes the centre piece of an open-arched courtyard, the copper beech and silver birch and liquidambar outside its walls?

Look out for the softly fountaining silver birch, enjoy the changing colours of the liquidambar, and admire the copper beech, knowing we might not always have the benefit of them. The copper beech at risk is the one shown below. It is on the corner of Bricket Road and the road to Waterend Barn.

A plane to be seen from afar

The plane admired by Patrick Remmington is on the edge of Verulamium Park. It is in the gardens of a house in Fishpool Street but is so close to the river that it seems to be in the park. As you come in to the park from the entrance by the bridge in St Michaels Street, the plane is in amongst the glorious bank of trees on the left. It is far and away the tallest of them.

> It is a huge and magnificent example with a nice shape including large lower branches which must compare very favourably with any London plane in the centre of London. I see and admire it every day whilst walking the dog and think it deserves some recognition after taking what must be 250-plus years to grow.
>
> Patrick Remmington

Patrick Remmington is not the only person who admires and salutes the plane: when I was walking the 'Cycle Ride for Historical Churches' with Norman Lavers, he pointed out the plane to me. He said that whenever he was near, he would make a detour to see the tree – as I have done ever since. Mr Lavers died in 2010.

Here is a photograph of the tree taken from within its garden in Fishpool Street. For a photograph looking up into the tree, see 'Verulamium Park within 'St Albans city parks".

Prospect's prunus and The Limes limes

In the gardens of flats 54-68 Prospect Road, St Albans, is a pair of trees of an unusual kind I have not seen elsewhere. Many people admire them. There were three trees, but they were drastically over-pruned in 1998 and one died as a result. They have pretty delicate pink blossom which comes early, followed by red leaves like a copper beech, then a round fruit like a big cherry but with flesh and stone like a damson. Birds love eating the blossom and ripe fruit. One tenant told me they were a Japanese tree and the fruit was inedible, another that the fruit is edible if boiled for a long time. Passers-by pick the fruit so I don't think it is poisonous, just not sweet. I have long wanted to identify these trees, and, if I move, I would like to grow them. I moved to St Albans in 1986 and the trees were mature then. The flats were built in 1929 so the trees are probably 30 years old.

Maxine Elvey(22)

The lime trees(23) at the entrance to The Limes are my favourite trees because they are beautiful – a lovely green – and they are such mature trees, and a landmark.

Carol Mulberry

A beckoning pine

Whenever I am walking home from the town up to Mount Pleasant, however I am feeling, the tree sort of pulls me up the hill, and says to me you're nearly home. Even when it drops all its needles and I slip on them, I don't mind – it's a beacon(24).

Ann Hollowood

THE REMARKABLE TREES OF ST ALBANS REVISITED

Pine with a beautiful shape(25)

My favourite tree is a pine in the garden of No. 97 Fishpool Street viewed from outside 122–130 Fishpool Street as you go down the Street on the raised pavement. It is my favourite because, although we cannot see the whole of the trunk, we can see the beautiful colour, textured bark and, above all, the elegant shape of its needles against the sky. A beautiful thing.

Madeleine Sansom

Matched poplars

Along the Ver in the Gorhambury Estate is a plantation of poplar trees. They can be seen from the Redbourn Road (A5183) and, if you walk along the section of the Ver Valley Walk that is a permissive path through the estate, you walk under them.

> For me, the trees are a link with the past: they remind me of how things used to be when most adults, my dad included, smoked cigarettes and used matches to light them. I have been told, you see, that the poplars were planted under the guidance of Bryant and May as a crop for making matches – but that by the time the trees reached maturity the bottom had fallen out of the market: lighters came along, and that was that for matches. Most of the trees have been left to grow on but some of them were felled in 2008. I wonder what their timber was used for. We shall miss the trees along the river if they all go.
>
> Anne Valentine

The poplars are truly beautiful – in different ways depending on the light.

Lady Verulam confirms: 'You are quite right: the poplars were planted for the matches market which then collapsed.

'We also have cricket bat willows along the river so, despite the felling of the poplars, there are and will be plenty of trees there.'

Both poplars and cricket bat willows have a faint blue to their green, the willows almost grey, nestling against the taller poplars further along.

There is also a line of lofty lime trees along that Gorhambury side of Redbourn Road. They are level with the Prae Wood Arms, closer to the road than the poplars are. They, too, are superb.

High tree in Highfield

It is a beautiful tree, approximately 30 metres(26) in height (about 100 feet) – rooted in my neighbour's garden but dominates my own garden and can be seen from some distance away. I believe that it may have been planted in the second half of the 19th century, when Wellingtonias were fashionable with the Victorians.

Pauline Barnes

This tree would have been planted at least a hundred years ago in the grounds of Hill End Hospital.

I love the way the foliage curls upwards and the cones swing gaily. In July the cones looked pale green from afar but were already made up of browning lozenge shapes outlined in bright green.

St Nicholas matched pair

A giant sequoia stands at each end of St Nicholas church in Harpenden town centre. The towering trees are visible from Church Green and Kirkwick Avenue – and from within the churchyard.

> They are prime specimens of the species *Sequoiadendron giganteum*. An estimate of their height is 100–120 feet and they are virtually identical. They cannot be more than 150 years old as the species was only brought to the UK in the mid 19th century.
>
> Andrew Smith

'Wellingtonia' is one of the names for the *Sequoiadendron giganteum*. Others are 'Sierra redwood', 'giant sequoia', and 'big tree'. The first seeds came to Britain in 1853 so it is not surprising that John Lindley of the London Horticultural Society named the tree *Wellingtonia giganteum* in honour of the Duke of Wellington who died the year before (Miles, 2006). Its name contributed to the tree becoming a 'must have' for grand Victorian gardens and parks.

Soaring sequoia in Sandpit Lane

Lisa Curry wrote to say that her favourite tree was the redwood in Sandpit Lane in front of the flats in The Dell. I asked her whether she could say why she had chosen it:

> I suppose I love it just because it feels so out of place! The huge, beautiful redwood in the middle of St Albans. I often wonder why it's there, if it got planted or if it just seeded the natural way and how old it is? It's a mystery! I suppose that's why I love it. I love the colour of its bark as well, that deep red colour is lovely.
>
> Lisa Curry

These redwoods are certainly tall! See that this one is twice the height of the three-storey building behind it.

A sweet chestnut in Hill Street

> From Verulam Road, drive down Hill Street in the next few days and, when you reach the place where you could park motorcycles, look left at the big tree 'in flower' now!
>
> THAT's my favourite, at my favourite time of year for it.
>
> Veronica Furner, on 9 July 2010

I am not sure why Veronica put 'in flower' in quotation marks. Could it be that she does not want us to expect something showy? To those unfamiliar with a sweet chestnut, the long creamy green strands might look as if they are foliage.

The tree is well set back behind the house but visible when you know where to look. Now that we do know, it will add to our pleasure when we walk along Hill Street.

A wide-spreading sycamore

When I asked a man whom I had met when he was doing charcoal burning whether he had a favourite tree, he drew my attention to this splendid sycamore that has been given the space to spread into its full natural range. It is on the corner of Waverley Road and Batchwood Drive – a busy junction of the ring road round St Albans – but I had never noticed it before.

I notice it now.

The scientific name for a sycamore is *Acer pseudoplatanus*. From the shape of its leaves and its winged seeds(27), we are not surprised that the sycamore is an *Acer*, the genus of maples. From its flaky bark, we are not surprised that it is a pseudo plane (genus *Platanus*).

Take time to enjoy the wonderful patterns of the bark. And do look up into the tree.

The Duke of Marlborough(28) weeping willow

I have chosen the weeping willow at the bottom of Holywell Hill because a childhood friend had a willow in their garden and I used to like going through inside. The leaves fell like a curtain and it gave me a magical feeling – like being inside a cave – completely surrounded by tree.

Kate Shuttlewood(29)

Willows are unusual, especially for a tree with catkins, in being insect, not wind, pollinated. This is a good adaptation because male and female willow catkins are on separate trees so that pollen blown by the wind might well not find a female willow catkin. Bees, on the other hand, can find the next source of nectar anywhere within a few miles and the chances are, at that time of year, it will be another willow. One drawback of insect pollination for early flowering trees is that insects need warmth to get them going. Willow fertilisation(30) therefore depends on sunny days in March.

Weeping(31) willow in Verulamium Park

The tree was a lovely little refuge for us when we were at St Michaels primary school. The leaves used to come right down to the ground so we would sit under it without being seen by the outside world! We used to sit and swing on its branches (without damaging them of course – we were very small!) for picnics and chats. It was a perfect little den for us :)

Lucy Crick

Lucy Crick and her friends are not the only ones to have loved playing under the willow skirts:

The willow tree is really beautiful. It is fantastically big and looks wonderfully peaceful and serene as you enter the park. It then however reveals a secret self and becomes a source of great fun for our family as the children love to run under its branches and play peek-a-boo, hide and seek, etc. We just think it is a great tree that looks spectacular and is fantastic fun. It has been there as long as I can remember and creates a lovely introduction to great parkland.

Jane and Dan Mountain,
members of the Cunningham Avenue Residents Association

The willow is on the right-hand side as you approach the lake from the Waffle House entrance to Verulamium Park. It is in fact three(32) trees whose foliage makes a perfect outline, as of a single tree.

Yews in the station(33) car park on Ridgmont Road, St Albans

In particular, it is the two yew trees in amongst a line of other trees, each fighting for elbow room, that inspire Philippa Parker:

> They are fine examples and are clinging on in this unbeautiful location, surrounded by cars. I hope they have preservation orders on them.
>
> Philippa Parker

Ivy is smothering some of the trees and they are all battling for light. The cedar's answer is to spread over the road, further softening the hard cityscape for us.

A yew at Norrington End

The yew tree(34) in the garden of the house next door to us in Norrington End is my favourite tree because it is very old and has an unusually positive shape for an English yew. Its girth is 4.7metres.

Kate Bretherton

On a bleak gloomy day in winter, it gives me a different perspective on life. Over the centuries our yew has seen it all: gloomy days like this come and then they go. My neighbour, Steve Mills, gave me one of his photographs that shows the yew on just such a day.

Trees that are history

Before the Grand Climax of St Albans most favourite tree, it seems right to tell of trees that are no longer there but are important enough in people's minds for them to write in and tell us about them. Peter Burley is one of the authors of 'The Battles of St Albans'. He wrote in to say:

> I think the most famous (perhaps the only famous) tree in St Albans is one that no longer exists and we don't know exactly where it was. Nonetheless I would commend giving it a mention. It is an oak tree, probably near the King Will, under which Henry VI sat obliviously singing hymns to himself while the Second Battle of St Albans raged around him on 17 February 1461. It does conjure up quite an image.
>
> Peter Burley

Have you heard the phrases 'eye-sore', 'safety hazard', 'in the way of the traffic'? There is nothing new. These were the reasons given for 'clearing away' an elm in Hatfield Road. When? 1907. The headline in the *Herts Advertiser* of 20 April 1907 was 'Last of the Mohicans'. The article referred to it as a 'traditional tree' and mourned its passing, but pass it did. At one time there must have been a number of elms in Hatfield Road and, to be called 'Mohicans', must have come to be bare-branched sharp-pointed remnants of their former selves. Mark Freeman, author of 'St Albans, a history', nominated this tree for inclusion.

> Many years ago there used to be a large tree in the middle of where Hatfield Road, Clarence Road and Camp Road meet, forming a roundabout. I can't remember what kind of tree it was, but it made a huge and wonderful impact on that area. There must be pictures(35) of it somewhere.
>
> Penny Jones

I can find no pictures of the tree. I wonder whether anyone else remembers it – and whether it was one of the 'Mohicans' and had to come down because it was diseased.

> Whichever way the sun is shining when the tree is in leaf it beckons like a shining beacon between the two fields.
>
> Pat Beaumont

Penny Jones tells us that Pat's copper beech is in the Napsbury Lane end of the hedge between the two fields at the back of Ayletts' Garden Centre on the A414, that it has been dying for some time (large amount of bracket fungus) and is now quite dead, and very unsafe. Strictly speaking it is on private land: the fields were the subject of a recent village green application by the local residents. Whatever the verdict on the open space, it sounds as if it is too late for the copper beech, but I so loved Pat Beaumont's description of the tree that I wanted to share it with everyone.

Although members of the current St Albans Mothers Union claim no knowledge of this next tree(36), Jim Cozens' description is so graphic that I want to share it, too:

> I came up to town one day for one reason or another and I saw
> groups of motherly-looking women – each group with a banner
> like the ones we see in church or carried by trade union members –
> processing up from the Abbey to town and round the old Town Hall.
> The procession was slow and silent and had power and impact. It was
> very impressive.
>
> Jim Cozens (born 1926)

My son Richard characteristically gave me his *least* favourite tree. It, too, no longer exists but he would not want not to hold on to the fun of his resentment against it. And he is not the only one, it seems, for the tree is the reason that St Albans City Football Club was denied promotion.

> During a second spell in charge [John Mitchell] took the Saints to the
> runners-up position in 1992–93 only to be denied promotion to the
> Conference at that time due to a 140-year-old oak tree standing within
> the terrace behind one of the goals. In 1998 the diseased tree was
> felled.
>
> www.sacfc.co.uk

St Albans most favourite tree:
the Abbey cedar of Lebanon in Sumpter Yard

More people nominated the cedar of Lebanon in Sumpter Yard close to the Abbey as their favourite than any other tree. It is an iconic tree: often, people would tell me about a personal favourite and then say 'and of course the Abbey cedar'. People tend to say the 'Abbey' rather than 'cathedral', I notice.

The tree has conflicting associations: one with the Abbey as all-embracing church of the martyr, the other with superstitious rituals that are unexpectedly widely known and long practised.

... as a well known and very public tree.

Jenny Faldon

It is a symbol of St Albans' history. Alban gave his life to save a Roman soldier – and became the first English Christian martyr. He was executed because he confessed his Christian faith. The tree is over 200 years old.

Anne-Marie Dawe

We nicknamed it 'the wishing tree' as you're supposed to hold your breath as you walk under its branches and make a wish. You're not allowed to breathe again until you've cleared the tree's branches (this sometimes means having to run the last bit if you haven't taken a large enough lungful of air!).

Lucy Crick

If you walk round widdershins (anti-clockwise) 7 times, you will see the devil.

Carol Mulberry

It's almost too obvious to mention, but I think this tree is magnificent!

Jan Lennon

...its age and beauty

Pam Smith

This is the bewitching tree. When you run around it anti-clockwise at midnight on Hallowe'en three times you get to see all the ghosts and undead of St Albans past.

Ivor Kellock

This tree has magnificent spreading branches which remind me of a mother duck spreading out her wings inviting her ducklings to come in and seek shelter and warmth. This tree seems to me to be

Opposite: St Albans' most favourite tree: the Abbey cedar of Lebanon in Sumpter Yard

inviting citizens to come and seek shelter and warmth in the church (cathedral) and its environs.

Richard R Blossom

In the early 1930s we children were told not to speak under the tree because it would be unlucky. It was a tradition. Perhaps it was a way of preparing the children to be quiet when they went into the church. It was also said that if you walked round it 12 times at midnight, horrible things would appear. Of course, none of us was up at midnight.

Jim Cozens (born 1926)

We were told at Hallowe'en that you must be quiet as you go under the tree or an evil spirit or a ghost would come out and get you. If you did make a noise, you would be safe only if you ran round it three times clockwise absolutely silently. Even now that I am 29, I still think of the story when I go past.

Steven Brooks

It provides a picturesque setting for our cathedral.

Reg Beer

I've attached some photos I took of it in December 2009 (the tree covered in snow) which I hope will explain why it is my favourite – but in words – ancient, majestic and almost part of the Abbey itself.

David Chadwick

Here is one of David Chadwick's photographs.

Here are two more detailed photographs of favourite trees.

...ves of the
...egated maple
...inated by
...ly Davies
...John Rae.
...tree is in
...passage from
...xhouse Gate
...umpter Yard.

...ranch of
...oak tree
...inated by
...Sankey.
...on Beech
...e Lane,
...eathamstead.

Our favourite trees revisited

(1) There are now more trees in Victoria Street! See 'New to the book'.

(2) Tom Thompson submitted the ash tree in the garden of 1 Lower Luton Road, Harpenden, as his favourite tree. When Donato photographed it in 2010, it had recently been drastically pruned. Here is a photograph of the same tree in 2018. It has perhaps not regained its former extent but has an attractive full crown.

Ash at 1 Lower Luton Road, Harpenden, in July 2018

At one of my talks, the lady who lives in the thatched cottage, Jacqueline Hall, said that she wished it was not there! I understand, and am sad.

(3) Colney Heath Treasure Tots gave permission for their original entry to be reprinted. Treasure Tots is still going strong.

(4) Mrs Meakin's tree is not an aspen, *Populus tremula*, but another species of poplar. Sorry. I was misled by its magical shimmering and rustling but there is no mistaking the leaf shape – or the lack of double direction-change on the leaf stalk, or the lack of myriad suckers so distinctive of aspen. There is an aspen within 100 yards of Mrs Meakin's poplar. Join one of the Friends of Bernards Heath walks to have it pointed out – and learn a great deal more life-enhancing information about the Heath.

(5) I am glad we have Robert Merrick's attractive photograph of a chalk face of Myrtle Cottage. The chalk has been covered by white render marked as if in stone blocks. The nearest source of the particular chalk in these walls, in the opinion of a chalk geologist, is Cuffley, not Totternhoe as we would expect.

(6) Sandy Norman, author of 'Sopwell: a history and collection of memories', met with the vicar of St Stephens church and David Alderman of the Tree Register to view and measure the cedar of Lebanon behind St Stephens church.

Sandy shares with us an email from David Alderman sent in February 2014.

'It was wonderful meeting you, the vicar and other Sopwell residents to see such a magnificent cedar tree. I am sorry that the oldest this is likely to be is c.1750 but it is still a very fine specimen and, out of 2000 we have recorded, this is in the Top 50 for Britain. Regarding its status as the largest cedar in Hertfordshire, this is all dependent upon whether a tree survives at Beechwood Park School, Markyate. Until this is confirmed your tree at our slightly reduced girth of 8.3m at 0.4m is second largest.

'On the Ancient Tree Hunt, I have now verified the record for you.

'The measurements of the St Stephen's cedar are as follows:

'Height: 19m
'Girth: 8.3m at 0.4m
'Crown spread west-east 30.8m
'Crown spread north-south 29.4m

'The crown spread is the most accurate comparable measurements we have from the 1925 account in *The Times*. The Rev JB Booth quotes the greatest spread as being 84ft (25.6m). The girth of 31ft (9.44m) at 6ft (1.8m) must have included much exaggerated growth from branches, although his later letter suggests not, as he disputes the 45ft (17.7m) girth tree in Charlton Park for this very reason. However, our measurement yesterday clearly proves he was also quoting an inflated girth! With quite a few of its low branches removed I don't believe we can glean any more information as to its growth from re-measuring it again at a higher height. If only he had also measured it closer to the ground!

'I called in at the cathedral and the cedar there is 4.96m at 0.4m.'

Sandy adds,

'[The meeting and David Alderman's follow up email] were a mixture of good and bad news. [The cedar] is not as old as we think. It's a mere 250 or so years old in [David's] estimation. Apparently, when cedars first came to Britain in the 17th century, they were not that hardy and were all wiped out by 1743 when there was a terrific storm. People planted a hardier type after that and ours is one of them. Cedars of this type are very fast growing. David described it as a cluster tree, multi-stemmed, and so it looks big with all the branches off the several trunks, a bit like a hedge. On the other hand, he said it is a fine specimen: a champion category C tree! It is big in volume and David described it as 'classic'. He was pleased with its condition: there was only one branch which looked damaged and this had a hole in it which was likely to have been made by a woodpecker.

'Regarding the Henry VIII story [that the King courted Anne Boleyn under the tree], David said this may have been started by the Victorians who liked to exaggerate rumours. However, quite often trees were planted to commemorate an event, so it could have been planted *because* of the story. Or, it could just have been planted to replace one of the less hardy cedars – the dates are right. We will never know the true story, but the pair of them [Henry VIII and Anne Boleyn] were around our area and they may well have done some canoodling under a tree in the vicinity.'

I was interested that nowhere was it specified that the cedar is a cedar of Lebanon, *Cedrus libani*. Alan Mitchell (Mitchell, 1976) says that what distinguishes cedars of Lebanon from other true cedars is that 'upper branches are level, and all branches layer out to extensive flat plates'.

What is your verdict? The crown of our cedar is very high so that plates have not been allowed to form. Would you say that the upper branches are level?

However, David Alderman did say that he had verified the record on the Ancient Tree Hunt, and there it does label the tree 'cedar of Lebanon'. Search on line for 'Ancient Tree Inventory'.

Our arm spans are a handy way to measure tree girth – if we stop mucking about for the camera

(7) Lady Verulam called me in reply to my letter asking for an update. She confirmed what was in the original book and answered some other questions.

Some cedars in Gorhambury have had to come down. A guest pointed out that one of them looked in need of attention and the experts confirmed that there was a risk of branches falling. With children playing beneath the cedars, it was a risk that the family could not take.

Here is a photograph of Donato on one of the cedars that had to be felled. We can see how great its girth – and what a job it must have been coping with its branching.

Some cedars at Gorhambury had to be felled

Lady Verulam went on to say that, yes, the red horsechestnuts in the avenue that leads from the Roman theatre towards the house, are known in the family as 'Uncle Bob's brollies'. Uncle Bob was keen on cricket and, as he walked up and down the avenue on his way to Lords, was glad of the shade. The trees have come near to the end of their happy lives. Their pink flowers have looked lovely each year alongside the white cow parsley (Queen Anne's lace, I prefer to call it) out

at the same time. The family has already planted pink hawthorn to take over from the red horsechestnuts - and maintain the attractive colour combination.

The Wellingtonias (*Sequoiadendron giganteum*) on the Estate had to have their tops removed but have regained their shape.

Hedges laid about ten years ago have matured and will be providing good cover for small mammals using the hedges as a woodland corridor to reach mates in a wider gene pool.

Still in Gorhambury but going back to the 17th century, 'Would you have me pluck out my own feathers', was Francis Bacon's riposte to the suggestion that he should sell Oak Wood, of which John Aubrey wrote, 'The oaks of this wood are very great and shady. His lordship much delighted himself here.' (Tomkins, 1967 p34).

es laid by
ato Cinicolo on
Gorhambury
e

New stems are 6
feet long one year
after laying

Francis Bacon was unusual in not wanting to clear woodland at this time. See More about Tree management for a description of changing attitudes to woodland through the ages.

(8) The weight of snow in December 2017 brought down branches of the cedar at St Marys, Redbourn. See 'Fallen trees' below.

(9) The red-blossoming trees in Sandridge Road, so strikingly alternating with white-blossoming cherries, are red-blossoming crab apple trees, not ornamental cherries as I blindly assumed. I do not know whether originally all the trees were cherries, but the red-blossoming crabs have been there for some time.

Here is a photograph showing the Sandridge Road trees in full bloom in Spring 2018. We see from the bark of the tree in the foreground, that it is a red-blossoming crab apple, not a cherry.

Sandridge Road
trees in Spring 20
and the huge felle
trunk of one of th
early cherry trees

There is no suggestion that white-blossoming crab apple trees will replace the white-blossoming ornamental cherry trees.

Also in the photograph, we see the trunk of a felled original cherry tree.

For more photographs of the felled cherry, see 'Fallen trees'.

The original cherry trees were grafted to (usually more vigorous) root stock. Look for the line of graft about 7ft (2 metres) up the trunk.

(10) The conifer in Cumberland Court is a cedar.

(11) St Stephens Parochial Church Council was advised that severe pruning was the only hope for the huge horsechestnut in the churchyard. We can see from the photograph taken in September 2018 that the tree is much reduced.

veteran
echestnut in
ephens
chyard in 2018

(12) In April 2011, I took a photograph of the magnolia 'in the heart of St Albans' behind the Council offices. We can see the tree covered in nothing but pale pink-white blooms – and a little of its setting.

olia in bloom
2011 in the
park behind
Council offices

(13) The monkey puzzle in Southdown has gone. We should not be surprised: it was a very large tree for the space in front of the house.

(14) Beaumont looked very different a century ago. I met Carol Parker on a guided walk 'Made in Fleetville' organised by Fleetville Diaries. Carol told me that, for the Beaumont Avenue Queens Jubilee street party, they had found some early photographs of their road and directed me to where they had been found on the Internet. I contacted the photographs' owner, Andy Lawrence, and he was pleased to let me share his photographs. Here is one of them.

Beaumont Avenue about a century a

To see more, go to YouTube and search for St Albans Past and Present to see current views of St Albans, Harpenden and Wheathampstead morphing into the same view in earlier times.

(15) In early February 2018, a gigantic branch fell from Mary Robey's tree in Woodland Drive. See 'Fallen trees' below for photographs and comment.

(16) Mark Slater writes in 2018, 'I often talk about the book with visitors to St Luke's vicarage garden. The two oaks remain a notable feature, though sadly the larger tree seems to be dying rather faster than the smaller one.'

(17) Ric Andrews expressed the thought that the oak tree in Hatching Green might outlast the house next to it. I am sad to say that Ric Andrews did not outlast the house or the tree. I think of him as I pass the tree whose dignity and wonder he brought to our attention.

(18) The Panshanger Great Oak continues to thrive and can be visited in Panshanger Park, a wonderful country park of diverse habitats and a huge

variety of wildlife. It is well worth a visit. It is open most days during daylight hours or until 6pm – and it is free. The entrance to Panshanger Park is via the Thieves Lane car park located just off the Hertingfordbury roundabout on the A414 near Hertford.

(19) St Albans Museum has been incorporated into the St Albans Museum + Gallery in the Old Town Hall, Market Place, St Peters Street. A façade of the former museum building has been retained as part of a residential development. Its name, Oak Tree Gardens, gives us hope that our Museum Oak will be preserved.

The loss of the biodiversity gardens we must mourn.

(20) The police officers have long been gone from what was the police station in Victoria Street. They are now situated alongside Council officers in the Council Building on the other side of the Arena.

(21) The fate of Penny's plane in the Bricket Road/Victoria Street car park is still uncertain. St Albans District Council now owns most of the land and buildings in this area which is known as the Civic Centre Opportunity Site (CCOS). As at May 2018, the specific nature of the development is not known. Whatever it is, it will have a huge impact on the City Centre.

(22) Maxine Elvey writes in 2018, 'I unfortunately had to move from my flat in Prospect Road in April because of family circumstances, but the red prunus trees are still there, and they brought me great pleasure during the 32 years I lived in my flat. My kitchen window gave me a good view of them in all seasons. They come into blossom early, before other trees, usually in March. I particularly enjoyed watching wood pigeons hanging upside down eating the pink blossoms. I took some photos, but not very good, in case you may wish to include them. What makes the trees special are the red leaves.

'Yes I would be happy to be included in the update.'

...ograph sent
...axine Elvey of
...eon amongst
...lossom in her
...us in Prospect

Maxine sent us a photograph of a pigeon in amongst the blossom on her trees. How well the grey-green sheen of the pigeon's head, neck and tail blend into the bark, branches and underside of leaves; and the magenta-pink of its breast with the magenta leaf tops and pale-pink blossom.

(23) What I had not realised is that the limes at the entrance to The Limes off Spencer Gate were in a line leading up to Heath Farm farmhouse, residence from 1871 of Jacob Reynolds (1835–1926),

The limes now in The Limes are the trees on the right

farmer, businessman and brickmaker. The house stood where 7 and 9 The Limes are now.

(24) When the property at the top of Mount Pleasant changed hands, the new owners applied for permission to remove the tall pine in its garden. The application was challenged, and permission was refused.

The tree is now often strikingly floodlit from beneath at night.

(25) An arborist once said to me that she loved to see how Scots pines 'went their own way' once they reached a certain height. I look for that, now.

(26) Pauline Barnes writes in June 2018, referring to the tree at the end of her garden in Highfield, 'The Wellingtonia is still doing well – the only difference is that it has probably gained even more height since 2010!'

(27) Sycamore seeds are in a Y shape. There is a y in sycamore, which makes it easy to remember.

(28) The Duke of Marlborough pub, for which a nearby weeping willow was named, has now been converted into a house or flats. It is the building facing downhill at the lower corner of Grove Road and Holywell Hill.

(29) When I checked with Kate Shuttlewood that I could reprint her original contribution to the book, she replied, that it would be fine to include her contribution even though her weeping willow had since been much reduced. I went to see it in July 2018. It is thriving, and I was taken with the extraordinary shape of its trunk.

Trunk of the Duke of Marlborough weeping willow in July 2018

(30) Most weeping willows, *Salix babylonica*, in Britain are male clones, according to Alan Mitchell (Mitchell 1976). He adds a note, 'Occasional female flowers on male catkins!' So all that lovely yellow pollen, whether carried by insects or wind, would be lucky to find a female flower in the British Isles.

Fortunately, asexual propagation of willows is particularly easy. A reasonably long cutting of one of the fronds, pushed into moist earth will soon root – and grow quickly.

well willow
el

Between the Sopwell Ruins and the River Ver there is a willow tunnel which children – and dogs! – enjoy running through. The willow tunnel is looked after by members of the Sopwell Residents Association and this involves weaving in new growth to keep it trim. I wondered whether it would be possible to curve the top bits down so far that they could be pushed into the soil and held in place so that they could take root!

See, also, 'Batchwood' to find out how useful it is that willows propagate so easily and grow so quickly that they have become an important biofuel; and 'Wheathampstead revisited' to find out how useful it is that willows woven into spilings to protect a river bank from erosion, take root and sprout.

(31) There are 'weeping' ash and birch trees and many others. We call them 'weeping' not 'pendulous', although their scientific name is often 'pendula'. I wonder whether their 'weeping' comes from weeping willows which were perhaps so called from Psalm 137, 'By the rivers of Babylon, there we sat down, yea, we wept, when we remembered Zion. We hanged our harps upon the willows in the midst thereof.' And, hence, 'I'll hang my harp on a weeping willow tree,' in the song 'On Top of Old Smokey'.

The Psalm probably gave rise to the scientific name *Salix babylonica*, which species originated in China, not Babylon. From its depiction on fine china, we ought not to be surprised that it is a Chinese tree. As Colin Tudge writes (Tudge 2005), 'drooping languidly over lakes and lazy rivers as if specifically intended for patterned tea sets'.

Salix babylonica has brown twigs and, Alan Mitchell (Mitchell 1976) tells us, is a 'rare tree of poor growth here [in Britain]'. Our own beloved weeping willows have golden fronds and are mostly *Salix x chrysocoma*, or 'Tristis', thought to be a cross between *Salix babylonica* and a form of *Salix alba*, the white willow.

(32) There are four trees, not three, in the group of weeping willows at the entrance to Verulamium Park from St Michaels by the river. It is obvious from

the photograph that there are four – and I have checked to be sure I did not jinx the group and have one die on us. In checking, I noticed how tall two of the willows are: they soar upwards in a most un-weepy way.

(33) St Albans City railway station is to undergo a major overhaul. Work was planned to begin in the Summer of 2018. The main change will be to the Ridgemont Road entrance to the station and we are yet to see if the trees in the car park will be affected.

Of course, of more concern to commuters than the trees is whether Charlie's Coffee and Company and The Pudding Stop vans are able to continue to operate from the station forecourt on the Ridgmont Road!

(34) The Norrington End yew has no bark. Donato and I were flummoxed. How does the canopy get its water and nutrients if there is no bark under which xylem vessels can carry them? We found that there is an inner yew tree within the shell of the trunk. No wonder it is difficult to determine the age of yew trees if they can regenerate from within.

Given its girth is 4.7m (15 feet, to put it into the units quoted), the tree could be 350–500 years old (Miles, 2006). How did a yew come to be here from the time of the Great Fire of London – if not from Tudor times? Norrington Farm farmhouse was next to the yew. I can find no record of the date of the house but the last tenant's grandson, John Bromley, tells me that the house was said to be Tudor.

The whole farm was expropriated to make way for the M1 motorway. The house was demolished in the 1960s.

John's father did a painting of the house, in the 1930s. We can imagine that the house has been around for centuries – and say that it was just the sort of place where a yew tree would be planted!

Painting of Norrington End Farm farmhouse

Steve Mills, the owner of the tree, tells us that rabbits make their burrows under the tree roots. Hmmm.

(35) Ian Tonkin read of Penny Jones' regret at the loss of 'a large tree in the middle of where Hatfield Road, Clarence Road and Camp Road meet, forming a roundabout. I can't remember what kind of tree it was, but it made a huge and wonderful impact on the area. There must be pictures of it somewhere.'

There *is* a picture of it! Ian sent me a post card photograph which Ian thinks was taken about 1914–15. It shows a spreading tree with a soldier standing in front of it under a sign post, railings round the tree, shrubs within the railings under the tree.

I cannot tell the species of the tree from the photograph. Can you?

The Crown Hotel, St. Albans.

(36) In my original text, I quote what Jim Cozens described to me a Mothers Union procession he witnessed. The quotation makes no mention of a tree planting! However, my memory is that the procession was to do with the planting of a tree in the Abbey churchyard.

St Albans city parks

St Albans has remarkable parks: snug little places tucked right into the heart of the city, one beside the Council Offices behind St Peters Street and Vintry Gardens behind the High Street; Clarence Park with its collection of Victorian specimen trees; the incomparably beautiful Verulamium Park in its lakeside setting and views of the Abbey above banks of trees; Victoria Park which is a model for community enterprise and commitment; Jersey Farm Woodland Park, which has lovely open countryside; Bernards Heath with its wilderness, woodland, parkland and open fields; and Highfield Park with its mix of one-hundred-year-old trees and new planting.

Vintry Gardens(1)

Vintry Gardens is down Waxhouse Gate right in the heart of St Albans between the High Street and the abbey. It is a walled garden and, until the 1970s, was the garden of a house in the High Street.

> 'Incidently, I always liked the *Ginkgo biloba* tree in the Vintry Gardens, it seems a bit out of place...'
>
> Elanor Cowland

Who could not like a *Ginkgo(2) biloba* anywhere. The common name is 'maidenhair tree' and it has a delicate pretty look with its special deeply-incised fan-shaped leaves, soft and velvety in whorls round each spur. The *Ginkgo* in Vintry Gardens is mature and magnificent. The interesting thing is that these fabulous trees are madly primitive. They are gymnosperms like cycads, yews and conifers. 'Gym' is from the Greek word meaning naked – ancient Greeks were naked when they did their workouts – and the seeds of gymnosperms are not clothed in an ovary as is the case for other trees, angiosperms. Another phrase I like in this context is 'motile sperms do the fertilizing': the distinction being that the pollen tubes of angiosperms have to burrow through living tissue down to the seed in the ovary whereas the pollen of gymnosperms 'exhibit [their own] motion'. There are fossil records of

Ginkgo biloba tree
in Vintry Gardens

Mulberry tree in
Vintry Gardens

THE REMARKABLE TREES OF ST ALBANS REVISITED

Ginkgoales 260 million years ago when the continents were still snuggled up together as one great supercontinent, Pangaea. Remember that fossil records of oaks only go back 60 million years when all the continents were well on their way to where they are now (Tudge, 2005).

Vintry Gardens is a popular place for people to go at leisure times. There are seats and lawns and wonderful old yews trees, a walnut on the Abbey side, the golden ash(3) in the top corner planted for the 'Year of Prisoners of Conscience' (see 'Paul Arnold's trees'), the attractive oak planted for adventuring youngsters who died in a tragic accident (see 'Trees with history'), an amazingly large hornbeam in the corner by the upper entrance and a wonderful old mulberry tree that bears good flavourful fruit. A path winds down via rounded steps through herbs to the lower gate out into Sumpter Yard.

Clarence Park

If you were a millionaire, what gift would you give to the people of your town? Something that would be for everyone now and forever? John Blundell Maple gave us Clarence Park in 1894. He bought the land from John Poyntz, Earl Spencer and a bit from Frederick Sander, the orchid grower (see the Mexican lime in 'Our favourite trees'), 25 acres in all. He bought 11,000 trees and shrubs, 300 species in all from W Paul & Son in Waltham Cross. He commissioned the local building firm of Miskin to build the pavilion and the lodge. He had laid out a cricket pitch, tennis and quoits courts, a football field, a bowling green and cinder tracks for running and cycling. He put in six hydrants to water the cricket pitch, and his wife, Lady (Emily) Maple, gave us an Aberdeen granite drinking fountain. Then as now, access to the park was free but people had to pay for using the sports facilities.

An avenue runs from the bandstand to the fountain

There is an avenue of maples, venerable planes and oaks from a bandstand to Lady Maple's fountain. The whole area around the avenue is the part of the Park devoted to specimen trees and there are some here that are seldom seen except in public parks: an euodia, a foxglove tree, a tree of heaven, a weeping ash and an oriental hawthorn.

The euodia(4), *Tetradium daniellii*, is in the corner by the 'away' gate of the football ground. It does not look frightfully impressive after drastic pruning, but no doubt it will come back to its full glory. The tree originates in China. It is famous for having no leafbud casing – the tiny folded shoot is surrounded only by dense red-brown hairs. An attractive thing about the euodia is that it flowers in autumn. After the drastic pruning, the only limb that carries flowers is very high but if we look up we can see fist-sized clusters of deep red flowers. And that is in September.

An euodia

The foxglove tree, *Paulownia tomentosa*, is the one with a sloping trunk close to the path that runs alongside Hatfield Road. It is next to an Indian bean tree. Both have floppy leaves and pale flowers in large panicles but the foxglove leaves have an extra point midway along opposite margins, the flowers are earlier (May not July) and are more mauve, and the fruits are in heart-shaped cases rather than the long thin pendulous pods of the Indian bean tree.

Between the Indian bean tree and the avenue is the tree of heaven, *Ailanthus altissima*. It has pinnate leaves, red on opening and then a lovely fresh green. The leaves are larger than those of an ash and each leaflet has a pair of pointy little lobes at its base.

Tree of heaven foliage and detail showing its crimson petioles

The oriental hawthorn, *Crataegus laciniata*, is only as oriental as Sicily. Its leaves are a prettily incised downy grey, and its fruits are downy orange-red. The one in Clarence Park is next to the tree of heaven.

The weeping ash, *Fraxinus pendula*, is impressive and is what it says on the tin: dense ash-like foliage fountaining out and down as does a weeping willow. It is alongside a bed of yellow roses over near the lodge.

Weeping ash

There are umpteen varieties of maples throughout Clarence Park, as one would expect when Maple was the surname of the man selecting the trees. Some of the leaves are deeply incised, some have hardly discernable lobes, some have great big seeds with wings spread across in a line, some have small seeds in a horseshoe pattern, some seeds are green, some seeds are red, some petioles are crimson, some petioles are yellow, some leaves are fresh green and some leaves are purple-brown, some trunks are smoother than others, some bark has twisting patterns. I would not want to spoil your fun trying to make out which variety is which – but take some headache tablets as well as your field guide.

Deodar branch tips droop. Dawn redwood foliage is dainty.

There are good examples of Atlas cedars, especially the ones by the lodge. There is a lovely deodar cedar with its languidly drooping branch tips on the lodge side of the bandstand adjacent to a conical dawn redwood.

There is a restaurant on the corner of Clarence Road and Hatfield Road and it opens on to the Park where we can sit out at tables. A waterfall of a grape vine over the walls and purple prunus trees round about make it pleasant. Next to the prunus trees and in amongst maples is a silver lime, *Tilia tomentosa*. It is a real wow! Dense foliage, silver grey underneath, abundant flowers and great height make this tree exceptional.

The silver lime contrasts with the greens around it

The photograph frontispiece of this chapter is of a tulip tree in Clarence Park. It is near the basket ball net not far from the zigzag up to Hatfield Road. It is a truly wonderful tree in every way. Lord Maple himself took some trouble to position it where it would get the right amount of sunshine and his care has been well rewarded. There is another tulip tree in the Park, within sight of the first, close to the fountain and within the avenue. Tulip trees have a distinctive leaf shape which reminds me of the

Tulip tree leaves

simplified dress shapes I cut out of paper as a child to fit round a cardboard doll. It is worth our while to find the tulip trees and admire them from afar and to look up into their divine heights. In autumn the whole tree becomes a tower of molten gold.

There is another special tree in Clarence Park. This time it is not in the area of specimen trees but at the corner of York Road and Clarence Road. It is a wych elm with a girth of nearly a metre and a spread the width of Clarence Road. It arches right up and over us as we drive along oblivious of being under an elm tree. Wych elms are relatively resistant to Dutch elm disease and this one shows no sign of being invaded. Andrew Branch, head of Trees and Woodlands at the Council, pointed me to the tree but how I had missed it is hard to imagine. I was fascinated by the early pretty maple blossom on trees along York Road but entirely overlooked the giveaway heaps of elm seeds in the gutter.

We nearly lost our elm. When I marvelled to a friend(5) about it he said that he had been asked to look into the problem of the awkward camber in the road at that corner. On inspection it was obvious that the tree and its root system caused the hump but my friend advised that nothing should be done about it because the awkward camber calmed the traffic speed and increased rather than reduced safety. Life can take interesting turns.

Wych elm in Clarence Park on the corner of Clarence Road and York Road

I have described just some of the trees in the Park. There are red oaks and red horsechestnuts, whitebeam, thujas and Lawson cypresses, stone pines along the Clarence Road fence from the lodge to the restaurant, an exquisite liquidambar near the pavilion, trees planted in commemoration: masses of super trees for us to enjoy – a truly remarkable park.

Opposite: looking up into one of Clarence Park's tulip trees

Verulamium Park(6) and Westminster Lodge

Wherever we took my late father-in-law, he had always been somewhere better. Not so with Verulamium Park. "I have never seen a lovelier park than this, Kate," he said in his measured Lancastrian voice.

Before we go into the Park at the entrance by the river in St Michaels, it is worth looking over the road to the far end of the Kingsbury Mill car park. The poplar there is amazingly tall and wide spreading.

As we come into the Park, we see a group of weeping willows, wide and, of course, pendulous. This group is seen as one tree and is a great favourite (see 'Our favourite trees').

Away to our left on the edge of the river towards The Blue Anchor(7) is a row of drastically pruned willows – they looked like stumps last winter but they have a bit of shape again now.

There follows a dense bank of trees along the edge of the river. See if you can pick out a plane tree amongst them, and go in under the branches and you will find you are on the edge of water, on the far side of which is the huge

Left: Poplar by Kingsbury Mill.

Opposite: The four(8) larches growing along the line of the Roman wall in Verulamium Park are iconic

Looking up into the great plane tree

trunk of that plane tree. Then look up – and up, and up to see the extent of this amazing tree. As you come out into the light you will be able to see the top of the tree above all the others. This is another of 'Our favourite trees'.

Look also for two conical-shaped trees with delicate fern-like foliage. These are dawn redwoods, *Metasequoia glyptostroboides*, and are, for me, one of the prettiest trees I know.

There are more lovely willows ahead on the edge of the lake, one weeping on the near side of the bridge and then a goat willow(9) on the further side of the bridge.

The lake and bridge and dense bank of trees along the river

There is a wonderful array of horsechestnuts, ash, sycamores and maples sweeping up and sometimes swooping down over the river. The Friends of Verulamium Park(10) tidy this stretch when it shows signs of getting totally out of hand. We can see some of the results of their work in sawn-off branches and piles of logs left for beetles important to the cycle of nature.

There is a whitebeam and a beacon of a Scots pine on our right and then many grey willow trees that look good from the other side of the lake, their light colour a foil to the rich green foliage behind.

At the end of the lake, we turn and walk along the lower level of the causeway, enjoying the reflections of the picturesque willow-covered island, a remarkable heronry.

As our path curves upwards, to the left there is an insignificant looking tree but I have my eye on it. It is a hawthorn and has good space around it which is unusual for a hawthorn, even in the countryside, where they are usually part of our hedges. I hope I am around in twenty years time(11) to see how it has shaped itself.

Through the trees to our left is Westminster Lodge. If we divert up the path a little we will be surprised to see quite a shrubbery and three robinias. This was the garden of the farm house that used to be here. Whoever lived here would have had a wonderful view(12) of the Abbey. If we raise our eyes we can see the generous bank of trees, mostly poplars along the bank of the Ver, and see, also, a group of poplars and willows round a modest brick building in the middle of the field.

Retracing our steps to the path we were on, we continue(13) in the direction we were going, leaving the lake behind us to go up the incline towards the fencing(14) round the foundations of the Londinium Gate of Verulamium. Horsechestnuts, limes and sycamores soar high to left and right on either side of the Gate.

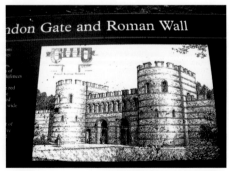

don Gate and Roman Wall

A horsechestnut towers as high as Londinium Gate must have done

The trees give us a measure of the height the wall and entrance gates must have been: on the Roman wall leading away from us we can see the layers of flint and mortar between rows of terracotta tiles(15). If we count the towers'

layers in the picture on the information board, and add them in our imagination to the layers in the existing wall, we can see that the gate would have been massively impressive – as tall as our massively impressive trees.

There is a pathway behind the Gate that crosses the extraordinarily deep ancient ditch. Watling Street to Londinium would have run from here to where St Stephens Hill meets King Harry Lane at St Stephens Church and then on as straight as a die to what is now Marble Arch. If we go a little way through, we come to one of my favourite trees, a mature sycamore(16) of splendid shape. Below the sycamore to our left is the circle of American trees planted to commemorate the founding of Rotary International in Chicago (see 'Paul Arnold's trees planted for their historical connections'). Above us is the Abbey View golf course with its striking trio of copper beech trees and pretty curved plantings of wild cherry, lovely in the early spring, and a good mixture of other broadleaf trees.

Returning to Londinium Gate and skirting its railings, we take the path(17) behind the Roman wall, now on our left. Gangly trees arch out towards our path. They are wych elms and, in April, have a mass of seeds that look like flowers. Feel how rough the leaves are: a characteristic of elm.

Elm seeds in April

The drinking tree mentioned in 'Our favourite trees' is on the slope of the Roman wall on our left, and from here on, within the curve of the wall, are wonderful specimen trees, well spaced so that they have reached their full height and spreading natural grace, or grouped in magical groves.

There are deciduous trees: oaks and beeches, planes, sycamores, maples and dainty hornbeams. The branch-bones make exciting patterns in winter, each with their distinctive leaf buds: pointed brown-red of the beech, small multi-bumps of the oak, swollen and green of the sycamore, slender and irregular of the hornbeam. In March there are swathes of yellow carpet from maple flowers, in April pink from beech blossom. In May there is still the tracery of branches on some trees, the tender copper of beech leaves, silver for grey willow and poplar underleaves, and fresh spring green for some others. In summer the trees are magnificent in their fullness, and in autumn the colours are spectacular: golds and reds and browns.

Beech trees in early spring – and a detail of maple flowers and copper beech flowers

And in amongst the deciduous trees are some very special evergreens. We come first to a group of tall cedars. There are four true cedars. For current purposes, we can ignore the Cyprian cedar because it is not grown much here. The others are the cedar of Lebanon, the Atlas cedar and deodar cedar. Even according to Alan Mitchell's field guide (regarded as the bible for tree identification(18)), the foliage of the different species of cedar is indistinguishable except at the branch tips. A supposed clever way to remember which is which is L for Lebanon and level, A for Atlas and ascending, and D for deodar and descending. We are not talking about the branches as a whole but of the new shoots – the very tips of the branches. All the cedars have barrel-shaped cones with a whorled indentation in the centre of the top. They are apple green in spring gradually growing more pink and then brown. It is a joy to unravel them after they have fallen to the ground. They come apart into lovely shapes, wide at the top then curving in then out then down to a point. They are velvety to the touch, tawny outlined in brown with a pale line across the wide part.

Opposite: In summer, a grove of copper beech trees is magical

Cedar trees

Consultants employed by the Council identified this first group of three as cedars of Lebanon, the distinguishing feature of which is the way the branches of mature trees form layers – making them utterly stately. Vic Coombs (Coombs 2004) identified these three as deodar cedars.

The next evergreens are a pair of giant redwoods, *Sequoiadendron giganteum* one much taller than the other, both with their distinctive conical shape. The two trees are down in a bit of a hollow, which lessens the effect of their height. They have dense foliage and splayed and buttressed bases that will become more so with time. See if you can find a cone. They are egg shaped, the size of a hen's egg or bigger, and I think they look as if they are covered in kisses from wide-mouthed 1950s puckered smackers.

In their area of origin, the slopes of Sierra Nevada in America, some of the trees are more than 3,500 years old. We do not expect trees here in England to be as long lived – but who knows?

A pair of giant redwoods

Giant redwood cone

Note that the trunks of the giant redwoods are unusually squashy and fibrous. They are fire resistant and the seeds in general only germinate after fire. The scenario(19) is something like this: terrible fire, all trees around burnt to a cinder, sequoia seeds burst from their cones onto ash-fertilised soil and start germinating in the ground below where there is lots of sunlight and no competition from other species. If the parent tree does die from the fire, all the better for sunlight for the seedlings.

Upwards from the sequoias towards the Roman wall are three superb Douglas firs. They have cheerful upward-lilting branches counter to one of the distinctive features of Douglas firs: the downward hang of their cones and yew-like foliage, soft to the touch. Another distinctive feature of this fir is the cones which have three points on each scale. Douglas firs are the tallest trees in this country. It is a native of North America but cultivated throughout Britain for its high quality timber. Here protected in the park, it might reach its estimated life span of 750 years (Coombs, 2004). What a wonderful legacy we leave for the generations to come.

Distinctive 3-point scales of a Dougla fir cone

The Latin name for the Douglas fir is *Pseudotsuga menziesii*. 'Pseudo' means false, and the English common name for *tsuga* is hemlock, not the poisonous herb, but a similarly towering conifer with yew-like foliage. Menzies is the name of the man who first discovered the trees in British Columbia in 1792, but it was David Douglas who successfully brought back the seeds from North West America in 1827, hence the common name. The seeds were nurtured at Scone in Scotland and a tree from one of those seeds survives today.

Douglas was a great character and intrepid specimen gatherer and kept an account of his adventures for us to read. He tells us that he risked his life in appalling weather, fell down a ravine, capsized in rapids, clashed with North Americans and several times nearly starved to death. But his end tops it all: he accidently fell into a bull pit in Hawaii and was gored to death. He was only 35 years old (Miles, 2006).

Look on our Douglas firs, marvel at Douglas and know that Douglas fir masts and spars have sailed the oceans and the trees have changed forestry in Britain.

The wide-spreading conifers that we come to next are six excellent Atlas cedars.

The first of them is a blue Atlas cedar but the ones on the other side are not so grey-blue in colour. The branches are wonderfully wide-spreading and the tree tops echo the peaks of the Atlas mountains from where they originate.

The scientific name for the Atlas cedar is *Cedrus atlantica* and it is also called the Atlantic cedar. The blue variety is var. *glauca*, one of the most planted of all decorative conifers.

Opposite: Dougla firs

Along the left side of our path has been the curving line of what was the Roman wall, densely wooded with beech, ash, oak, sycamore and maple. If we go up onto the wall alongside the Atlas cedars, we see the amazing network of the roots of beech trees. The prominent remains of the Roman wall come to an end with a huge beech. If we go round to the far side we see(20) across a slope down and then up to a line of mature trees interspersed with such smaller hedging stuff as blackthorn (white with its pretty blossom in March), hawthorn (white with mayflower in May) and elder (cream with umbrate flower heads in June) all along King Harry Lane. If we go up to where there is a gap in the line, we see an amazing tree stump as wide as I am long. It must have been an absolutely massive beech tree. We can see the substantial logs from it on the ground nearby.

Atlas cedars have wide-spreading branches

Roots of beech trees on the Roman wall

As we turn our backs on King Harry Lane and look over the Park we have a breathtaking vista of wide grassy space, mature standards, the lake below, the bank of trees above it up to the town, and the Abbey far right. We are fortunate to be here.

As we walk down the hill, we note how the trees ahead are in a line across the park. These mark old field boundaries. See how the whitebeam stands out pale against the oaks, beeches and sycamores on either side. To the right of this line of trees, beyond the white hypocaust building, are the stone pines planted to commemorate

Whitebeam foliage is pale grey

the Roman temple (see 'Paul Arnold's trees planted for their historical connections'). The stone pines have a distinctive umbrella shape which marks them out from the other pines around them.

We cross the line of trees only to see another line across ahead. In this line, away to the left, is a single larch in a line of good, spreading, sycamores, and an especially majestic sycamore on the boundary. This turns out to be a pair of sycamores whose canopies have spread to make them look like one tree. Their bark has formed beautiful swirling patterns.

Ahead is the hedge round Verulamium Museum car park, which is an absolute picture in spring with luxurious bowers of dense white ornamental cherry blossom.

On the left, just through the hedge, is the 'ladies gate' into St Michaels churchyard and through the car park is Verulamium Museum.

However, if we turn to walk along the path on the park side of the hedge, we can explore more of the Park. When we come to a path by the tennis courts we can turn left towards the Inn on the Park, and on down towards

Cherry trees in the Verulamium Museum car park in April

THE REMARKABLE TREES OF ST ALBANS REVISITED

the lake. Along the lake side we shall find a soaring double-crowned lime tree, a prettily shaped silver birch, a wonderfully ancient London plane allowing its lower branches to sag, a super group of horsechestnuts, six beeches – two green, four copper – and, near the play pool, a group of maples and then a group of cherry trees.

And so we reach the lake edge and have to choose our path home.

Jersey Farm Woodland Park

Open countryside in Jersey Farm Woodland Park

Jersey Farm Woodland Park is an idyllic stretch of open countryside and woodland between Sandringham Crescent and a field short of Sandridge. A board at the entrance, where Chiltern Road joins the Crescent, tells us all about the history of the area and that '10,000 trees have been planted including 800 as a millennium project in November 1999. 16 London planes have been planted at the four entrances. Among the trees planted here are alder, ash, beech, crabapple, holly, hornbeam, larch, lime, oak, pine, poplar, silver birch, and sycamore.'

Not only are there the trees listed above but also hawthorn, blackthorn, cherry and rowans in a great wild bushy hedge. Within the shelter belt of the trees and hedging, grass stretches away, with white daisies or whichever meadow flowers are in season, giving us long views over to Sandridge.

It has been a most successful use of land for the community, the trees protecting the Park from traffic noise and pollution – a great big natural open space for us to enjoy.

Victoria Playing Field(21)

I could take a bet and be sure to win that at least half of the people reading this will be wondering which is Victoria Playing Field. And yet we all know it. It is the triangular space above the point where Verulam Road and Folly Lane meet. There is a garage together with a tyre and exhaust fitter right at the point and then the Playing Field.

Victoria Playing Field in evening light

It might seem like a bit of left-over space, an awkward shape, difficult to do anything with, which was just left open. Not so. There was a plan to move Aboyne Lodge School into the space but local people convinced the Council that they valued the Playing Field as it is. Since then, the Friends of Victoria Playing

Saturday morning football in Victoria Playing Field

Field have made great strides in fulfilling the community side of the bargain: to really make sure that the Playing Field gets used to its maximum potential as a recreation area. There are 'Larks in the Parks' with story-telling, games and hands-on arts and crafts; 60 boys play football each Saturday morning; there are fun football and cricket events and the local nursery school brings children down to help with tree planting.

There is something of a tradition for Victoria Playing Field to keep up. Would you believe that after the Crimean War there was a one-armed, one-legged cricket match here? I presume that some of the participants had lost a limb – or two – in the war and the other participants temporarily immobilised a limb – or two – to make the game fair. That's the spirit!

Friends of Victoria Playing Field have been good about planting new trees. Tim Leicester is determined to have a tulip tree but has twice been given something else. There is a hope that wild cherry trees and two sweet chestnuts will provide future fruits and that two horsechestnuts will provide conkers.

Someone planted a weeping willow for their mum, and someone transplanted a little hornbeam from their allotment. As well as the wild cherries, the Friends have planted ornamental cherries, *Prunus kanzan*, which have deep pink blossom in dense clusters, and bird cherry of which there are already some in the Playing Field. The bird cherry has much bigger leaves than you would expect a cherry to have: as long as 10cm and 7cm wide, on grooved short red petioles and with sunken veins. Flowers are in pendulous buddleia-like sprays and fruits are black and spherical. I know all this because I did not recognise the tree and had to carefully note its characteristics and look it up. Another new ornamental cherry has been planted: a great white. Is it so called, I wonder, because as we stand under it looking up at its intense white blossom it is like being under the belly of a great white aquatic predator?

When we say that the Friends have planted the trees, we should say that they have bought – or acquired – the trees, the Council contractors have dug holes for the trees and then the Friends, usually with the help of Muriel Green Nursery School children, have planted the trees. After that, a Friend of Victoria Playing Field 'adopts' the tree: keeps an eye on it and meets any needs – like extra watering – when necessary.

So much for the new trees and the future, but already the Playing Field is rich in mature trees. As we come from the top Verulam Road entrance we are under a London plane. Its leaves are such a bright green and it is such an airy tree that even in the evening there is no feeling of gloom under it. Next to it is an even more venerable plane. Its girth is nearly 4 metres (390cm, to be precise) and it is probably the age of the houses along the road. They were built in 1840.

There are attractive maples, some strikingly variegated green and cream. One on Verulam Road catches the eye, and Donato has captured in his photograph, opposite, one bathed in a shaft of evening sunshine.

There are loads of lime trees and they all have flowers sparking off in different directions. According to Alan Mitchell, this is distinctive of small-leafed limes, one of our native limes (Mitchell 1976).

And we must not fail to mention a super oak on the Folly Lane side, or the wild meadow being 'cultivated' in the lower part of the Playing Field. This is to encourage little animals, insects and wild flowers and herbs.

In the same spirit of biodiversity, when a substantial tree died, the Friends thought it would be good to leave it there for woodpeckers and beetles and agreed with the Council that this would be the right thing. The Friends had just planted some wild clematis to climb up it, blinked, and whoops! The tree was gone: the Council contractors had cut it down. The clematis has grown well and the Friends have extended the stump with a bit of trellis to amplify it.

This is altogether a lovely park, well cared for by everyone concerned, and ours to enjoy.

An oak in Victoria Playing Field

THE REMARKABLE TREES OF ST ALBANS REVISITED

Bernards Heath

There are several different parts(22) to Bernards Heath, each an exceptional community resource. There are two fields where we can play wide games and youngsters and dogs can run about; there is wild parkland, some of it more wild than others, some of it more parkland than others; and there is woodland.

Upper Bernards Heath is a wide open space along Sandridge Road

The top field – or upper Heath – is beside Sandridge Road(23), lined with the alternating red and white cherry trees that commemorate the Second Battle of St Albans. Within the open space is a fenced and hedged playground with brightly coloured equipment for children to climb and swing on and slide down. The lower Heath is adjacent to the upper Heath down a short slope through a line of trees on the far side from Sandridge Road. We shall come to that later.

An exceptionally graceful maple at the corner between the upper heath and wild parkland

The trees along the town-side edge of the upper Heath, between the asphalt path and the houses, are pleasant and spreading and there is a particularly attractive maple(24) in the corner at the end of the path. It has wonderfully wide slender curving branches and tiny shrimp-like flower buds in April.

If we go through that corner of the upper Heath we come out on to the end of Heath Farm Lane and across from it is part of the wild-parkland of Bernards Heath. There used to be a dairy farm here and most of this area was grazed until the 1930s. It is interesting to think that all that we can see and are about to see has grown up since then.

We cross Heath Farm Lane and take the left-hand path into the wild parkland area. At first we are within a belt of very tall ash and poplar trees (see Mrs Meakin's poplars in 'Our favourite trees'), and then come out into a magical space, mown but otherwise untamed. There are lovely hornbeams, a

Through a belt of very tall trees we come into a magical mown space

natural small leafed lime in the corner to the left, and a beech tree ahead on a path leading us away to the right. We follow that path by the beech into more wild and wonderful vegetation – lots of elders with their large umbrella-shaped white flowers in May and glossy sprays of purple-black berries in September – and then follow a path to the left that takes us out onto Harpenden Road.

My next-door neighbour in Walton Street, Ella Bevan, was born in 1904 and she told me that she could remember the cows lumbering across the road here to graze on the other side. We shall do as the cows used to do and cross the road – with care because drivers put their foot down to get up the hill and do not seem to notice that the road has levelled out and the extra acceleration is no longer required.

We are now on the west side of Harpenden Road in more formal parkland. To our left is a wonderfully wild wilderness – definitely worth a wander some other time – but we shall go straight ahead under the big maples and huge

A flowering maple in more formal parkland west of Harpenden Road

Blossom on the gigantic bush outside Spinney Cottage

beech to a gigantic clump of what looks like blackthorn but is in fact a species of plum. It is a mass of white flowers in April and has sweet dark red fruits in September.

Spinney Cottage is behind the plum and we go right on the track outside the house, down into the woodland section of Bernards Heath.

We soon see the deep dips from which clay was extracted to make bricks. Local people refer to the pits as 'the bumps' but they are more than that, a perfect natural playground for cyclists who love to speed down and up the long steep slopes under tall trees. Trees are most substantial along the left edge of this strip of woodland, but are all large enough for us to marvel at them being less than 80 years old.

Our path comes out onto Harpenden Road close to the Ancient Briton and we cross over onto the path opposite that takes us up the hill through a mirror image of the strip of woodland we have just left.

Towards the top of the path(25), we pass the Lombardy poplars at Heathlands School and come to the complex of Judo Club, Pioneer Club, old fire station and ambulance buildings. We go left behind them on to the lower heath, cross the space or skirt it, and aim for the path through the far line of trees.

At the top of this path between lower and upper heath, we come to a tree that is worthy of comment. It is a sizeable oak that Jennifer Faldon nominated

An oak between the upper and lower heaths. It is older than any of the other trees nearby

as her second favourite after the Abbey cedar. It is particularly significant here because it is obviously considerably older and more substantial than the others anywhere on Bernards Heath.

We have been within a stone's throw of the centre of town and yet in open space, parkland, wilderness and woodland. St Albans is a remarkable place.

Highfield Park

Highfield Park is where the former Hill End and Cell Barnes hospitals were. There are some magnificent trees here planted when the hospitals were founded at the end of the 19th century, and the Highfield Park Trust has

done an inspirational job in preserving the trees, creating a village green, commissioning works of art, providing recreational areas for picnics, football, cricket, boules (petanque), providing children's play equipment – and planting exciting new trees and creating a Tree Trail round them. It is all mapped and explained in an attractive leaflet(26) available from the Trust offices within the Park at West Lodge.

We shall follow the Tree Trail and discover its interesting trees, but in amongst the housing there are also amazing trees. In 'Our favourite trees', we were introduced to the giant redwood in Russet Drive, and outside the Trestle Arts Base we can see a beautiful set of mature trees. As we walk through the streets of Highfield we can look out for more of them – and perhaps take a stroll up to the Hill End Garden of Rest between Hill End Lane and the Alban Way cycleway and footpath. The small cemetery is something of a wilderness but mature trees spread over the indistinct little grave stones in a sheltering way.

The Tree Trail itself starts from a path leading out of the car park behind the shops on Hill End Lane. Significant trees are marked by a distinctive disc with a number that relates to interesting snippets of information on the Tree Trail leaflet. I do not want to steal the Trail's thunder, but do look out for the wonderful old London plane and old robinia to the left of the

A purple sycamore stands tall between a sweet chestnut and a cedar with the old robinia lurking behind

path at the start of the Trail. Each has bark that is knobbed and humped and grooved to a ridiculous extent. Neither bothers much with a canopy, unlike the common lime and purple sycamore between them and the red horsechestnut(27) and copper beech on the other side of the path.

The Trail takes us to the edge of an orchard and then, in case we slip through the orchard onto Hixberry Lane and then to The Plough at Tyttenhanger, it slides us sideways past a new holm oak and a European larch into an attractively wild part. There is a mown path for us to follow and it leads us to a big turkey oak, a giant redwood, a deodar and the Indian bean tree nominated as a favourite.

A red horsechestnut has interesting branching, and still a few leaves in late November

Mown paths
lead us round
the Tree Trail.
Here we see a
giant redwood
and the Indian
bean tree
nominated as a
favourite

We curve right round to another giant redwood and then two particularly attractive trees planted by the Trust: a dawn redwood and a swamp cypress. These trees each have dainty feathery leaves, the swamp cypress branches curling round like a dog trying to make itself comfortable in the blankets of its sleeping basket. The swamp cypress, the Trail leaflet confirms, can produce

Leaves of a wild service tree in the inner circle of the Village Green

pneumatophores, breathing roots, more handy in a swamp than at Highfield but who knows what climate change will throw at us.

The Trail then takes us across the bit the Trust is calling the Village Green. It has an inner circle of newly planted wild service trees, *Sorbus torminalis*. Rowans (mountain ash) are of the same genus but have a pinnate leaf, quite different from the lobed but entire leaf of the wild service. This is a native species but is not mentioned elsewhere in this book although most other native species are referred to many times over. The Trail leaflet calls it 'the forgotten tree of the English landscape' and it must have been more widespread than it is now because a drink, checkers, was commonly made from its fruit. The drink was so popular – or perhaps easy to make from ever-present trees – that many inns or pubs specialised in it and took their name from it. Most of the pubs called Chequers have a chess board on their pub sign but that comes from not knowing the origin of the name.

The outer circle of the Village Green is of hornbeams and in amongst them and outside them are self-seeded trees, oaks and other natives, and it is hoped that eventually we shall have native woodland surrounding the Green.

The Tree Trail takes us on along a line of oak trees planted by Groundwork Hertfordshire to commemorate the planting of 100,000 trees through the county following the great storm in 1987, and then takes us on across Hill End Lane into another great lobe of Highfield Park.

At first we go parallel and close to the road, past a lovely silver birch and on to where we cross Highfield Drive and go into Winchfield Wood with its mature oaks and some coppiced hornbeams. More native trees were planted here in 1997 to 1999 and it will be good to see how it all matures.

Apple trees in the old Cell Barnes Hospital orchard, trained along a fence line

After a good stretch, we cross Highfield Drive again and into what was the Cell Barnes orchard. The information board(28) that tells us all about the orchard was not there when I passed recently but we can see apple trees trained along a fence line.

After the orchard there is a Norway spruce (our traditional Christmas tree), a pair of blue Atlas cedars(29) and then a splendid beech tree by a maze with a winged totem at its centre.

Before we go forward to cross Highfield Lane back to the car park and reality, it is worth taking a moment to find the lines of ash and oak near the great beech. The lines mark old field boundaries and remind us how areas adjust and develop over the centuries according to our changing demands. Given that we have introduced extensive housing here, we have done well to retain attractive trees and plant many more.

St Albans city parks revisited

Vintry Gardens revisited

(1) Kate Morris has written 'The Vintry', a history of Number 3, High Street, St Albans. Elizabeth Rolfe collaborated, focusing on the history of the gardens and stableyard and tells of the ownership and uses through the ages. It makes fascinating reading. The booklet is available from its publisher, St Albans & Hertfordshire Architectural & Archaeological Society.

(2) The name 'ginkgo' is a Japanese derivation of the Chinese yin-kuo, which means 'silver fruit' (Miles, 2006).

(3) The ash tree planted to commemorate the Year of Prisoners of Conscience has been replaced by a strawberry tree, *Arbutus unedo*. See 'More about Paul Arnold's trees'.

Clarence Park revisited

(4) The euodia, *Tetradium daniellii*, in the corner of Clarence Park by the 'away' gate of the football ground is still looking unimpressive. The larger of its stems has been cut through low down. Its innards do not look healthy. Maybe the rest of the tree will continue to support a reasonable, if very high, crown. What is certainly good news is that a new euodia has been planted nearby.

Euodia   Bee Tree
15.1.57 - 30.1.15
In memory of Bob Keane
who loved to walk his dog
Biffo in this park

Dedication at the foot of the new euodia

It has a dedication plaque at its base, and will be forever cherished by Bob Keane's friends and family.

I described how, in 2010, I could see, in the crown of the euodia high above me, 'fist-sized clusters of deep red flowers'. It is the *seeds* of the euodia that are 'red-brown erect pods'. The flowers are 'dull white with

The new euodia is the sapling on the left, the old euodia in the central corr to the right of a flowering Robinia

sexes on separate inflorescences on broad-conical heads 10–15cm across'. I am agog! Will the new euodia develop quickly enough for me so see these amazing sights, I wonder.

(5) The friend who was asked to look into the awkward camber in the road at the junction of Clarence Road and York Road is Terry Hill. He lives in St Albans. I wonder if he thinks of his happy decision as his vehicle wallows over the lumps caused by the roots.

Verulamium Park revisited

(6) A map shows the route of the walk I describe through Verulamium Park.

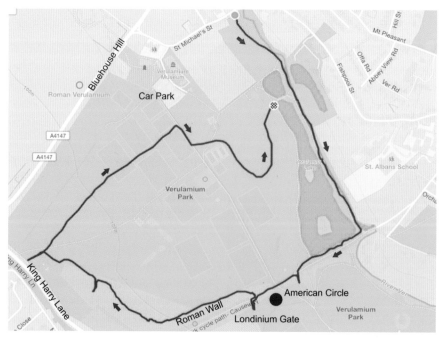

Verulamium Park showing walking route

(7) The Blue Anchor is now a private residence but retains the pub sign.

(8) There are now three larches, not four, along the line of the Roman wall.

One fell in the Winter storms of 2018 and the 'others will continue to be assessed as part of the rolling programme of tree safety survey'. The trio looks as iconic as the quartet did, but we are reminded of their vulnerability.

For my Hello Trees books, Donato and I took photographs of the flowers of these larch trees. Their colour and shape delighted us.

Female and male larch flowers

(9) I labelled the willow in Verulamium Park at the end of the bridge between the boating pond and the lake, a goat willow, *Salix caprea*, also known as 'sallow' and 'pussy willow'. Willows hybridise easily so that it is difficult to be sure of their species. It is certainly a willow tree, and certainly a female and *probably* a *Salix caprea*.

Pussy willow brings to mind our much-loved furry, silver-then-yellow

catkins. The female catkins, have their own beauty. If you look closely, you will see whirls of teeny discrete female flowers, each with their own perfect, purple stigma to which the right pollen will adhere; a slim connecting style; and a gently bulging ovary. The whole is fronded with fine, shining, silver hairs.

Female willow catkin in April

I like to have forays to look forward to and shall visit the tree in April to see whether the tree's flowers are the same as other willow female flowers that I have seen at that time of year.

If the female catkins get pollinated, tiny flask-shaped seeds surrounded by woolly fluff are released into the air in late May, leaving remnants of arching styles.

I have a photograph of our catkins in June. Clinging to them are the remnants of seeds, proof that our catkins have been pollinated, but goodness knows where the pollen comes from.

Have you seen a male pussy willow tree anywhere near by?

Flowers of the willow by the bridge in Verulamium Park, June 2013

(10) The Friends of Verulamium Park has disbanded. Its remaining funds are held by the Ver Valley Society, to which most of the former Friends now belong. Do join us. We have a delightful website that gives all details of events and how to join. It won't break the bank and its events and information are a treat.

(11) I expressed a wish to see, in twenty years' time, how a hawthorn tree at the end of the causeway in Verulamium Park had shaped up. Ten years on, it does not seem to have changed a jot! Hawthorn branching is very dense. The tree has probably increased in density rather than height or width.

(12) From ground level in Summer it is hard to see through shrubbery to the Abbey, as I hoped the people living in the farmhouse on Mud Lane close to the causeway would have done.

(13) As we walk past Mud Lane and up the incline towards Londinium Gate, Dr L E Perrins tells us that the line of sycamores on our left 'marked the old boundary between the Gorhambury estate and Verulam Fields Farm. Most have small leaves and are the variety purpureum. Those with large leaves are the normal variety. Sycamores are supposed to have been introduced by the Romans. It is interesting to speculate that these trees are the direct descendants of the original introduction' (HMTNC, 1982).

Alan Mitchell confirms that sycamores were 'introduced probably by the Romans' but writes 'Jersey 1828' against the variety 'purpureum' and makes no mention of it having smaller leaves, only that the leaves are 'dark purple beneath tinged grey' (sic, no commas) (Mitchell, 1976). This is unsatisfactory from a scholar's point of view but, for me, the idea of a border between a farm and an Estate being marked in our Park by sycamores is attractive.

We can indeed see large sycamores in a line right up the hill. Some are alongside the circle of American trees (see 'American trees for Rotary beginnings' in 'Paul Arnold's trees') Some are close to the fence on the Westminster Lodge side of the Roman ditch. Their leaves are neither small, nor purple or grey underneath - or above. And there are sycamores everywhere in the Park, so who knows whether these are our boundary markers, but it is enjoyable to explore and speculate.

Dr Perrins goes on to tell us that the 'shiny red pustules on the leaves of sycamores and other maples are caused by gallmites, and the tarry black patches on sycamore by a fungal infection' (HMTNC, 1982). So, while we are boundary-spotting, we can add to our interest by distinguishing between gallmite and fungal infestations.

Tired by the hill climb? There is a bench at the top. It overlooks the golf course, the superb trio of copper beeches, wild cherries, amazingly tall trees along the line of the Roman ditch - and a most unusual view of the Abbey's south face. Pause a while.

(14) Most of the fencing round Londinium Gate has been removed but you will know when you have reached Londinium Gate.

(15) I am informed that between the layers of flint in the Roman wall are terracotta 'bricks', not 'tiles'.

(16) One of my favourite trees was a mature sycamore with a splendid shape as illustrated. It was up the hill from the circle of American trees, on the line of Watling Street close to Londinium Gate. There is absolutely no sign of the tree, only a dome of elder, nettles, thistles and self-seeded wild cherry saplings.

(17) The Council has been mowing broad paths through the grass and, if you follow the mown path, it will take you on the walking route described.

I thought I had misheard when a Verulamium Park contractor first told me about ecotones. I thought he said 'zones'. 'No, tones as in the tone of your voice,' he corrected. Ecotones are the areas of wilderness between and on eitherside of the mown paths.

The definition of an ecotone is 'a region of transition between two biological communities. 'Ecotones between two habitats are often richer in species than either' (https://en.oxforddictionaries.com/definition/ecotone, OUP). 'Tones' in this context comes from the Greek *tonos* which means 'tension' ie the line where the two communities are in tension (ibid.).

Ecotones don't make much sense to me in a park: the wilderness areas all seem to have much the same ecosystems of wild flowers, small mammals and insects, so there is no 'tension' between them, and the mown paths cut them off from each other rather than providing a place to meet. However, it does makes sense to me that the mowing provides a comfortable path for walkers, keeps walkers confined to limited routes and allows wildlife to thrive elsewhere.

We are glad, for every reason, to follow the mown paths.

(18) Paul Arnold was my mentor when I wrote the book in 2010. He regarded Alan Mitchell as the ultimate authority on tree species identification and I still refer first to Mitchell's field guide (Mitchell, 1976). However, classification systems are being challenged (Tudge, 2005) by DNA mapping and I tend, second, to search online to check that there isn't a note about the species having been re-classified. It seldom has. It is interesting that the early systems of classification based on grouping together organisms with like-characteristics, has been a good indicator of the evolutionary relationships confirmed by DNA mapping and, for the most part, early classification holds good.

(19) In their native California giant redwoods are well adapted to withstand moderate fires – in fact dependent on them to flourish. Before the gold rush of the mid-19th century, moderate fires started by lightning strikes would clear the brush from around the trees and stimulate the cones to release their seeds. Since then, firefighters have put out fires and flammable brush has grown up, putting the trees at risk of more dangerous larger and hotter flames. The so-called Ferguson Fires of 2018 in Yosemite National Park in California were so rampant and so hot and the smoke so dense, that firefighters had to race to protect the 1000-year-old giant redwoods.

(20) As we come out into the light from being under the canopies of specimen trees, we are about level with the end of a stretch of vegetation-topped Roman wall. If we go to the tall beech at the end of the wall and keep curving round to the left, we overlook a long meadow between the wall and King Harry Lane.

Again, we have a broad mown path, an 'ecotone', to lead us around the meadow in an ellipse avoiding damaging the wildernesses on every side.

Then, to get a good view back over the Park, we have a choice of mown paths radiating upwards to our right. Any one of the paths will take us up to the line of trees that edge King Harry Lane.

I did hope that I could re-find my massive beech stump along this line, but it is nowhere to be seen. Nor are the 'substantial logs from it on the ground nearby'. It is interesting to see how vegetation moves in and comprehensively covers all that is beneath.

Victoria Playing Field revisited

(21) During the exceptionally long hot summer of 2018, excellent volunteer watering efforts kept alive new trees in Victoria Playing Field, the triangular open space above the point where Folly Lane and Verulam Road meet.

Even a new hedge-tunnel that the Friends of Victoria Playing Field had planted has survived. The hedge tunnel joins up strands of trees behind the play area to provide a natural play feature. This is the ultimate addition to the new natural-look (mostly wood) play area that was built in 2017 following a crowd-funding appeal.

Friends have also planted a hedge of native trees along the Folly Lane boundary, replacing non-native laurels.

A cherry avenue on one side and an arc of cherries on the other make the Playing Field a must-visit place in Spring. Some of the cherries have been donated by members of the public in memory of relatives or, in one case, a beloved dog.

The planning, care taken over materials in the playground, memorial plantings and the conscientious care of the trees are evidence of the importance to the community of this lively open space.

Bernards Heath revisited

(22) We ought to include Beech Bottom Dyke when we consider Bernards Heath. It is on the north side of Beech Road from the rest of the Heath but the grazing area of the Heath probably extended to the edge of the Dyke where we can see evidence of a laid hedge.

The Dyke is a Scheduled Ancient Monument, an Iron Age, mile-long earthwork, a deep wide ditch, significant in the strategic decisions made in the Second Battle of St Albans.

If we start opposite the Ancient Briton on the corner of Harpenden Road and Beech Road, we see larches, pines, oaks, and every kind of hedging tree. It is only just possible to traverse the Dyke edge from this end but there is a path further east along Beech Road that leads into the Dyke at the point where earth has been built up in the ditch. We can see where the earth was taken from because the space along the edge widens out. Here are the beech trees that give Beech Bottom Dyke its name. From here we can walk along the edge of the Dyke to where it reaches Valley Road.

In Spring, bluebells are a picture within and alongside Beech Bottom on either side of Valley Road.

(23) For more about the alternating red and white blossom on the trees along Sandridge Road, see 'Our favourite trees revisited'.

Also, I need to be careful to explain that the trees 'along Sandridge Road' are on the Sandridge Manorial Wastes as distinct from Bernards Heath. The Wastes, as we call them, were granted for the grazing of livestock being driven to St Albans market. The livestock (cows, sheep, geese?) could do with being rested and fattened after their trek if they were to fetch a good price.

The Wastes were owned by the Manor of Sandridge. The manor in turn was owned by the Abbey of St Albans 796–1539 and then by secular owners. Before the Peasants Revolt in 1381 the Abbey seems to have charged tolls to use the Wastes. These were lifted, and that may be the only enduring success of the Revolt. They are, and always were, commons and are separately recorded under the Commons Registration Act, 1965. To protect them, they have their own set of bye-laws (formalised in 1915) which vary from those for the rest of the commons on Bernards Heath.

(24) The maple at the end of the path along the town-side edge of the upper Heath is a silver maple, *Acer saccharinum*. It has a great bundle of mistletoe hanging from its branches. Look out for mistletoe on the Heath. There is quite a bit of it on one species of tree and another.

(25) On our way up the path with the Ancient Briton behind us and Harpenden Road on our right-hand side, there are trees on either side of us, remarkably large oaks on our left. Also on our left, is the Ariston Site, which, as of 2018, is destined for development. It includes the lower Heath field and what was the complex of Judo Club, Pioneer Club and old fire and ambulance station. However, there is no suggestion that we shall lose the upper Heath field, nor the trees and open spaces of the rest of Bernards Heath.

Heathlands School with its Lombardy poplars is well set back from our path. That is to stay.

It is a good 100 yards/metres diagonally across the lower Heath field to the gap in the trees where the short, steep climb is up onto the upper Heath field by the sizeable oak tree.

I need to say that the oak is considerably older and more substantial than the others, not 'anywhere on the Heath' but rather 'than those nearby': there are sizeable oaks alongside the path up Harpenden Road, as described in the paragraph above.

Highfield Park revisited

(26) The Highfield Park Tree Trail leaflet can be downloaded from http://www.highfieldparktrust.co.uk/tree-trail/. As at 2018, the pale green 'download here' within the text is easily missed – but it is there and will offer you the leaflet.

A super new visitors' centre was opened in July 2018. The Highfield Park Trust can be contacted there. It is near the junction of Hill End Lane and Frobisher Road.

(27) The original red horsechestnut in the Highfield Park Tree Trail has been felled. A sign directs us to another.

(28) The information board at Cell Barnes orchard has been replaced. We are told of the history of the ownership of the orchard, the different ages of the trees, the different varieties of fruit that were grown, about two of the different ways fruit trees were trained against fences – and how the grass is cut only twice a year so that a wilderness can develop and aid biodiversity.

(29) If the handkerchief tree that died, number 29 on the 2018 version of the Highfield Tree Trail, is replaced in the same position, it will be on the same side as the blue Atlas cedars, opposite the Mediterranean cypress.

Opposite:
Bark texture and branching are a delight in our park and open spaces

St Albans churchyards

Abbey churchyard(1)

St Albans most favourite tree, the cedar on the Sumpter Yard side of the Abbey, and its young descendant on the north side; the wonderful beech tree at the northwest corner; and the delightful variegated maple at the east end have been spoken of in other chapters. There is also a handsome yew in the corner by the door into the south transept, and a glorious lime tree in the circle of grass at the west end.

Opposite:
Beech tree in the
northwest corner

Right: Lime tree
at the Abbey west
end

St Peters churchyard(2)

Cedar of Lebanon and other trees in St Peters churchyard

St Peters churchyard(3) is the lungs of St Albans – it keeps us all breathing in our busy city centre. It is at the top of our main street tucked behind a trafficky roundabout and is a haven of calm and refreshment.

St Peters church has been re-thinking the role of their churchyard and, at the festival of St Peter in 2010, partners in St Peters Churchyard Community Project outlined plans to foster biodiversity and create a place of beauty and possibility, a place of remembrance and reflection. That sounds like a place where each and every one of us can go to be revitalised – and be welcome.

Entering the churchyard from alongside the gardens of the war memorial, we come into an avenue of limes and yew trees. By going right, we pass a car park that has been well designed to allow grass in amongst little concrete squares: 'grasscrete'. It is surrounded by shrubs and trees.

On our left is a fig tree, drastically pruned in 2009 but showing good leaves in spring 2010. As we near the southeast corner of the church our eyes are drawn left to an ancient cedar of Lebanon that puts our own short precious lives into perspective.

The churchyard has many of those tall solemn conifers(4) that look at first very much the same as each other, but it is worth looking again. The first tall conifer on the right is a Western red cedar or *Thuja plicata*. It is

Tall thin conifers

not a true cedar (genus *Cedrus*) so to avoid confusion scientists prefer not to use the common name. Look in summer for the tiny cones. Spindle-shaped and upright, they are only a centimetre high but there are usually masses of them and they are an attractive contrasting yellowy-green until they turn brown in late autumn. Try putting the leaves to your nose. Do you smell pineapple? The aroma is a distinguishing characteristic of *Thuja plicata*.

Some of the conifers have a look of layers of candlewax dripping downwards. If they have grooved bluish chickpea-shaped beads on their leaves, they are Lawson cypresses(5).

The conifers at the end of the churchyard have much more swirly cheery foliage and some have abundant orange-pink flowers.

The Garden of Hope in St Peters churchyard

Paths cross at a horse-chestnut at the entrance to the Garden of Hope, named for the sentiment expressed on its stone sculpture: 'God is with us' we are told on one side, and 'There is Hope' on the other. There are plans for a mediaeval knot garden round the sculpture. Nathaniel Cotton's walnut (see 'Paul Arnold's trees planted for their historical connections') sways welcomingly above and beyond the sculpture. Remembrance services are held here and we see at the far end the small stones commemorating people whose ashes have been interred in the Garden. The low wall has been repaired and beds of herbs and vegetation low in height and in maintenance will be planted in the raised bits, and benches made and placed in the recesses. We can sponsor the benches. Leave a note at the office on the other side of the church (the north side, between the church and the octagon room), or speak to the vicar or churchwarden, perhaps at one of the church's delightful Wednesday lunchtime concerts.

Coming out of the Garden of Hope and turning left, the churchyard opens out for us. Set well back on the left is a tree with glossy deep-green leaves. It is a stupendous bay tree that mocks the clipped little ornamental lollypops outside restaurants. Go near and smell the leaves.

In front and beyond the bay is an area to be left to develop naturally, a

An aromatic bay tree in St Peters churchyard

place for meadow flowers and wildlife to thrive.

The rows of young cherry trees on either side of the path are pretty with pale pink blossom in Spring. The trees were planted and are maintained by the Clifton Street residents. Thank you: a gift to us all.

Young cherry trees in St Peters churchyard

The apple orchard to the right of the path was the inspiration of David Curry. 'You don't have orchards in churchyards,' someone said to David. 'You do in this one,' he replied. The trees are coming on nicely despite some careless strimming round their rabbit guards. The oak in the centre was planted for Gracie Lawrence who worked at Ryders Seeds. She ran St Peters church youth fellowship for 40 years.

Gracie Lawrence's oak in the centre of St Peters churchyard apple orchard

As we turn back towards the church and take the right-hand path on the north side of the church and octagon room, we come beneath my favourite ash trees, branches flinging themselves outwards and upwards, freely and joyously.

And then we meet the path that runs parallel to St Peters Street. Almost everyone walking to or from town in this direction cuts through the churchyard to be away from the roar and fumes of the road. The bench on the path usually has a mum or two with pram or buggy, or a shopper having a breather. On the left of the path after

the bench, the trees round the Garden of Rest make it a shady haven of peace. A coppiced hazel(6) and great lime tree draw us on towards the lichgate and then we are back to limes and yews at the way out to the town – and another reality.

St Stephens churchyard

In 948, Abbot Ulsinus built a church on each of the main roads into the town. St Peters in the north, St Michaels in the north west and St Stephens in the south on the road in from London.

St Stephens is an exquisite little church, made to look small by the absolutely wonderful horsechestnut(7) on its south side. Words cannot do justice to its calm soaring spreading magnificence. To stand under it and look up within it is to come close to that which is sublime.

St Michaels churchyard

There is some interesting stuff in St Michaels churchyard. As we come in from
the car park through the Ladies Gate – I love it – we are under a huge lime
on our right and an English yew on our left. Beyond the yew is a holly tree
of exceptional height. Slowly, slowly it has grown up and up and up into the
sunshine. Notice how the leaves further up are not so barbed. Barbing takes
energy that is not worth expending on leaves that are high enough to be out
of the reach of browsing animals.

Looking towards the church we see clearly the difference between English and Irish yews: the Irish ones are darker and have upward-pointing branches like very tight candelabra and are the ones that lend themselves to topiary(8).

We turn along the path before the church, and the cedar of Lebanon ahead takes our focus. It is old and spreading and just as it should be.

Beyond the cedar on the path out towards Bluehouse Hill, our eyes are drawn to a massive red and grey trunk on the left of the path against the brick wall. This is a Western red cedar, *Thuja plicata*. It soars heavenward, as does the next tree to the right of the path. This is a coastal redwood, *Sequoia sempervirens*. It is a magnificent specimen of a beautiful tree. The foliage is distinctive and delicate: see how the leaves go in and out in waves like a necklace, and the branches have a jaunty lilt at their ends. In their native California the permanent sea mists keep the trees supplied with moisture and they grow to be the tallest trees on the globe. The *sempervirens* in their scientific name means 'always living' because it is unique(9) amongst conifers in being able to regenerate itself after being cut down, rather like the hornbeams and hazels and other broadleaf trees after coppicing. They also sometimes take root after they have been blown down, and branches that fall off can start an independent life of their own.

Behind the coastal redwood is a collection of birch trees. They are not silver birches: their leaves are bigger and darker and their bark has a paper-thin white skin that peels and curls back. They are Himalayan birch trees, *Betula utilis*. Where there are scars on the trunk, there is a lovely rich red-brown colouring.

If we retrace our steps and follow the path under the great cedar – the paves of the path are grave stones – we see an interesting thing: on a plane tree, there is a branch from one stem to another that has completely fused to both. I have seen this fusing forced in mulberry trees in Agios Nicholios in Crete giving an arching cloister effect to the central reservation of a busy street, but it is not often we see it happening naturally. Here it looks as if the tree is offering to be a ladder for us.

Notice a sycamore tree that looks as if it has many stems. This is probably formed by growth from the base of a much older tree in the centre, now long gone.

A branch has fuse to two stems

THE REMARKABLE TREES OF ST ALBANS REVISITED

rish yew and
edar tree by the
ate to the village

With the church on our right now, we have three lovely cedars of different ages. The one nearest the gate is a particularly lovely shape. From St Michaels village it is a landmark, a life-affirming graceful culmination to one of the most attractive streets in St Albans, the prospect of which reconciles us to leaving our churchyard sanctuary.

St Albans churchyards revisited

Abbey churchyard revisited

(1) The cathedral is embarking on a landscaping project which will run up to and beyond the opening of a new entrance and welcome building on Sumpter Yard in Summer 2019. The initial focus will be on Sumpter Yard itself, but the plan extends to the whole curtilage of the cathedral. Present trees (most notably the cedar in Sumpter Yard) will be conserved, and many more added.

It is hoped to restore the medieval Abbey's 'Magnum Pomarium' – the Great Orchard – on the lower half of the land below the cathedral's south side, and there will be more planting in Sumpter Yard, the North Churchyard, and around the Deanery, with biodiversity very much in mind, as well as repair of dilapidated pathways and signage.

I checked with the Dean that Princess Diana's cedar would be preserved, too, and he said it would. He promised also to make a note to invite the monarch to plant yet another cedar on another quarter of the Abbey in 200 years' time.

St Peters churchyard revisited

(2) There are now information boards in St Peters churchyard. They tell us variously about the history of the church and about the historical associations and the ecology of the churchyard.

(3) St Peters churchyard is indeed 'a place of calm and refreshment'. I hope you did not think that I meant the kind of refreshment offered by a cafe!

In August 2018, retracing the steps described in pages 162-165, I think it worth mentioning how much of the planning has come to fruition.

The orchard and wildlife wilderness are doing well.

(4) Distinguishing one conifer from another was tricky for me – still is – but I have come to grips with the basics and have written it all up in a series of resource sheets that will always be available free from http://hellotrees.co.uk/resources/. See 'Conifer basics', 'Botanical names of conifers', 'When is a fir a spruce?', 'Why is a yew a conifer?' - or even 'KS1 Y1 Lesson Plan for January: larch, conifers'. The resource sheets, 'discovery sheets', are written with youngsters in mind. There is no need to be proud: simply find a youngster with whom to explore conifers.

(5) The scientific name for Lawson cypress is *Chamaecyparis lawsoniana*. We can tell from the genus that, despite its cord-like leaves, it is a sham cypress (genus *Cupressus*). To add to the confusion, another common name for the Lawson cypress is Port Orford cedar. It is not in the genus *Cedrus* either.

The other part of the species name, *lawsoniana*, is not for the man who introduced the tree into Britain but for the seed firm Messrs Lawson in Edinburgh to which William Murray sent, in 1854, the first consignment of seed from the valley of the Sacramento River in northern California. William Murray had gone to northern California to search for the distinguished Scottish botanist, John Jeffrey, who had vanished without trace while on a collecting expedition (Readers Digest Association 2002). The plant hunters had to be extraordinary people.

Alan Mitchell (Mitchell 1976) tells us that the crushed foliage of the Lawson cypress smells of resin and parsley. I don't get it myself. What do you get?

(6) Could I really have mistaken a lime for a hazel! There is no coppiced hazel to be seen near the lichgate in St Peters churchyard but there is a lime with multiple stems probably acquired after very low coppicing. Between the multi-stemmed lime and the lichgate are three good maiden trees: a lime, an oak and a hornbeam. On the far side of the gate, still within the churchyard, is another good maiden lime. A 'maiden', by the way, in this context is the term for a single-stemmed tree. Hmm.

The limes and yew making a guard of honour to the south door of the church are on our left. Ahead is a tall sycamore right against the churchyard wall. It can be seen from well down St Peters Street.

It is fun, and tempts us to look closely at all the detail, to compare the current view of St Peters churchyard trees to those in the photograph of the unveiling of the War Memorial in 1921.

The unveiling of the War Memorial in 1921 © St Albans Museums

St Stephens churchyard revisited

(7) The horsechestnut in St Stephens churchyard has iconic status amongst St Albans residents. The vicar of St Stephens Church, the Reverend Becky Leach, understands this and noted it in her press release on 31 October 2017:

HISTORIC TREE IN DANGER

The landmark horsechestnut tree that has stood in St Stephen's churchyard for over 230 years is suffering from a life-threatening combination of diseases that have weakened its structure to the point where action must be taken. The tree is situated on the south side of the church, close to Watling Street, and to ensure public safety the diseased branches will be removed and its height reduced. It is hoped that this much loved tree might then have a chance to recover.

Planted on 22nd November 1785, the fine horsechestnut tree in St Stephen's churchyard has become a well known landmark to visitors to the city entering via Watling Street. In common with most horsechestnuts in the area, it is suffering from an infestation of leaf-miner moth, but this is not the main cause of concern. The major branches of the tree were pollarded in the 1970s and serious rot and fungal infection has entered the tree from these points. Removal of diseased timber and reduction of height is essential to prevent loss of the entire tree and danger to those entering the churchyard.

Rachel Johnston, who is supporting the St Stephens Parochial Church Council on environmental concerns, adds, 'It's a pity that we don't have the date of the very tall lime tree in the churchyard. It, too, is a prominent feature of the skyline.' The lime tree's height is especially noticeable as we come along King Harry Lane towards the Church. 'Lift up your eyes', I say to myself.

St Michaels churchyard revisited

(8) Francis Bacon (1561–1626) of Gorhambury is said to have 'objected strongly to topiary, which he called 'images cut in juniper or garden stuffe, they be for children.'' (Wittering, 1983)

(9) I do not feel confident in asserting that the coastal redwood, *Sequoia sempervirens*, is *unique* amongst conifers in being able to regenerate itself after being cut down. What I can do is confirm that it can be coppiced vigorously, and that big stumps can produce a circle of new trees (Mitchell, 1976).

Very tall
lime tree in
St Stephens
church yard:
'a prominent
feature of the
skyline'

The drive into
Batchwood

Batchwood

In Batchwood there is ancient woodland, post-war plantation, wonderfully varied mixed woodland and fine landscaped parkland – all on the same site within St Albans, and open to us all.

As we turn into Batchwood from Batchwood Drive we are in an avenue of maples of different ages interspersed with a few sycamores. The spread of the branches makes a rounded enfolding avenue, welcoming rather than imposing.

At the top of the drive we find ourselves under thrillingly tall trees. Most are limes but there is an occasional sweet chestnut and, if we look into the dense natural mixed woodland on the other side of the drive, we see a very tall ash tree(1) disappearing into the sky. It is easy to locate because it is directly behind

Old ash tree

the red-disk 'no entry' sign. Look well on this ash tree because it is very old and may not stay upright much longer. There are signs of burn damage on it but it is its age rather than injury that makes it vulnerable. When the ash comes down it will let the light through and different plants and little creatures will come in and thrive. Although I shall mourn the lovely tree, it would be appropriate if it fell in the Year of Biodiversity, 2010–2011.

We walk on and note Roma Mills' robinia on our right by the wall (see 'Paul Arnold's trees planted for their historical connections'). Ahead is the tulip tree planted to commemorate the last mayoralty of the City Council (see 'Trees with history'). You can imagine coming up the drive and seeing it a beacon of molten gold ahead.

As we pass Batchwood Hall, the house Lord Grimthorpe built for himself, and turn left alongside it, we find ourselves under a group of three wonderful beech trees close to our path – too close for the health of their roots, so savour the trees now(2). In April, their flowers spread a pink carpet across the grass under the horsechestnuts and sweet chestnut alongside.

A carpet of beech flowers from three beech trees spreads under the two horsechestnuts and a sweet chestnut alongside Batchwood Hall

The golf course is like traditional English parkland

As we reach the end of the Hall, an evergreen holly oak stands sentinel and we turn left under it, onto a path in front of the Hall.

What a wonderful open vista of landscaped parkland we have here. To the right a copper beech is set before the avenue of limes and horsechestnuts that line the drive down and away; still right, but on the near side of the fairway, a sweet chestnut stands proud of a whole collection of large trees running into the distance; in line across the front of the Hall are a spreading oak, Lord Grimthorp's plane, a red oak, an elegant silver birch and a huge holly; and

THE REMARKABLE TREES OF ST ALBANS REVISITED

to the left there are wide-branched conifers near, a towering sequoia further, and a bank of Scots pine, birch and beech beyond. There are wonderful contrasting textures and heights and blends of colours in the trees.

Near to hand, in the right-hand corner beyond the putting green, is a small building clad in slabs(3) of elm. With most English elm trees gone, there will be few buildings in the future like this one.

At the end of the Hall, we come to a pair of fine oaks and turn right. The lumpy tree on our right is an ancient mulberry tree.

At the end of the line of rhododendrons on our left are groups of cedars and other specimen conifers and broadleafs. I especially like a silver birch that is more stocky than usual.

Mulberry tree

Group of
specimen trees

The broad path(4) into mixed woodland is one of my favourite paths anywhere. We shall come to good oaks on either side; an ash, a beech and a venerable horsechestnut in quick succession; paths and glades to the side, sunshine through trees to parkland, bluebells at our feet in spring and golden leaves in the autumn. And always we are aware of the awe-inspiring height of magnificent trees, majestic and calm with age.

Horsechestnut on one of the best paths anywhere

Our path was made for us by the Friends of Batchwood. The Council has responsibility for managing the whole site but it is ably assisted in looking after the woodland by the Friends of Batchwood(5).

In the picnic area(6) on the left of the path is a willow, one of the varieties developed for the quick growth that makes it an ideal biofuel.

Miles Soppit of Friends of Batchwood shows us the type of willow grown for biofuel

Squirrels have torn the bark from this young oak

An ash with a strip of its trunk peeled back

When grown specifically for biofuel, willows are coppiced and within three years will have grown multiple shoots ten feet tall and be ready to be coppiced again. Some shoots are retained for further propogation. They are cut into nine inch lengths and buried up to the last inch in soil. In three years they, too, will be ready for coppicing. The cut shoots are dried and burned, the energy used directly for heating or to generate electricity, in the process releasing only the gasses absorbed from the atmosphere during growth. Our own Rothamsted Research in Harpenden is working on developing the best willows for the job.

There is another willow behind the one at the entrance, and next to it we see an oak tree badly damaged by squirrels. It is heart breaking to find a strong sapling like this to be so injured after ten years of good growth. A humane squirrel trap is an attempt to keep the problem within limits(7).

Further along our path on the right is an ash tree that has a great strip of its trunk peeled back. This is like looking at a hedge-layer's work in magnification: see how the growth continues along the peel because the channels that carry sap up and down the tree are just under the surface of the bark.

We come to an opening on the right with a bench(8) at the base of a huge oak tree. Look up at the oak and you will see that a good half of it has been torn away. This was done by the massive beech tree we see(9) lying where it fell. In late autumn, the fruits of the fungus that did for the beech can be seen on its stump and all sorts of fungi along the log. We have lost beeches in Verulamium Park to the same fungus and there does not seem to be anything we can do to prevent it.

Much of the oak was torn away by the falling beech

To see(10) the coppicing done by the Friends of Batchwood and the hazel baskets they made to protect new growth, look out for a path on the left that has a particularly tall Scots pine at the far head of it. The baskets are on the right a short way up this path, some baskets of smaller stems, some using large and small stems. The Friends of Batchwood have done the kind of job that our ancestors would have done for millennia until the mid 20th century (see 'Tree management').

Fungus on the beech stump

You might notice an elm(11) between the two kinds of baskets. If it is the right season, look for the typical round seeds of the elm and/or the lopsided leaves that feel rough and rustle with a paper-like sound when you feel them. If there are no leaves or fruit, look for a tree with a strong shoot growing alongside. The bark looks unaffected by Dutch elm disease and Paul Arnold has identified it as not an English elm but a Dutch elm which should be relatively resistant to the disease. Let us see whether it matures.

Fine-woven hazel baskets to protect new growth after coppicing

Dutch elm with a shoot adjacent

Creatures make use of tree stumps

By carrying on we come back to our original path and continue under soaring trees. The path ends in sycamore after sycamore in a lofty line. A six-foot stump beneath them is home for all sorts of creatures. We saw bees coming in and out of one hole, but presumably the holes have been made by different creatures for different purposes over time. It makes me think of apartments on four floors.

Out we come onto the drive. We could go straight over the asphalt and follow the path on the other side, but I suggest we go left and, as the drive curves left, cross it and go on to the path that has a yew tree hanging over it from the right. Note the yew hedge going off up the drive – I wonder if this yew escaped upwards from the hedge.

Beech that started life at the time of the Battle of Trafalgar

From the path, look up hill to the right and see through the trees an exceptionally beautiful beech tree(12). It has a girth of nearly 5 metres and must be more than 200 years old.

We come to a bench on the path (where the other path comes down). To the right are oak and ash trees that are particularly tall and straight, and a sweet chestnut so tall and straight that it does not have the usual distinctive twist to its bark.

Further along the path we come to deep buttresses at the base of an oak, a Turkey oak(13). The buttresses are a distinctive feature of Turkey oaks, as are their mossy-cupped acorns and the regular squared plates of the bark with redness deep in the grooves. Our tree is massive with a groove right up one side.

A turkey oak

THE REMARKABLE TREES OF ST ALBANS REVISITED

We come out alongside an avenue of maples adjacent to the car park

Onwards and upwards we go passing new planting that is doing much better than in the glade at the bottom of the hill, and come out onto the edge of the golf course alongside the car park. The maple avenue here is a gem. Batchwood people call this 'Paul's leftovers' because Paul Arnold rescued the trees from the City Council's New Greens Nursery when it closed.

It is easier to get into the car park – or to continue on our Batchwood tour – from the other end of the avenue, so up it we go. The first trees are our native field maples(14) with smaller leaves and seeds, then alternating red and green non-native maples. In the spring, we walk on a gold carpet of maple blossom.

It is decision time: we can either call it a day and quit now by curling back into the car park, or we can go on for a circuit round the northern woods.

Within the avenue of maples

We in St Albans call this whole area 'Batchwood', but it is divided into two properties and so far we have been in the first property which consists of the golf course, the mixed woodland on either side of the drive up to the Golf and Tennis Centre, the Golf and Tennis Centre itself and Batchwood Hall. All this is now owned for us by St Albans District Council. Lord Grimthorpe left it to the City in his will. The second property is north of the first one on the other side of the strip of golf course behind Paul's leftovers, the tennis courts and the gym buildings. It is part of the Gorhambury estate.

If we decide to go on, we shall find that there are three distinct parts to the northern woods. You can see their different natures on Google Earth(15): a conifer plantation damaged by fire in the 1960s, the undamaged part of the conifer plantation, and ancient woodland. The parts are adjacent and edged along the northern boundary by what was once a laid hedge.

From the end of the maple avenue, we go to the right of the trees ahead, towards some high netting that protects the houses from flying golf balls. There is a pair of quirky conifers here. They have long tufty whiskers and an elegant long thin green cone. They are Bhutan pines, *Pinus wallichiana*, a 5-needle pine. Look closely at the needle bases and you will see that the needles grow in groups of five.

Bhutan pine cone

Look back and see the typical shape(16) – tall and narrow – of a lime tree at the start of the trees we are passing, and compare it to the spreading lime ahead. Tree identification by overall shape is tricky.

We pass the spreading lime, go behind the netting and then, at the end of the netting(17), prepare to cross the fairway. We look left to be sure we are not disturbing golfers and that we are in no danger of flying golf balls.

There is a clear path on the far side that takes us into the wood and then we turn left. We are now heading west(18) and, from here to the west end of the wood, we have the first of the three distinct sections of the wood:

Clear path into the northern woods

THE REMARKABLE TREES OF ST ALBANS REVISITED

the section of conifer plantation damaged by fire in the 1960s. At first we are surrounded mostly by conifers and then we find that there are different trees as nature has taken its course and filled in the spaces left by the fire. There is the inevitable sycamore, ash, and in some places silver birch. Towards the west edge of the wood, there are clearer patches created by the fire but

The section of the plantation affected by fire: silver birch has come in to fill some of the spaces

sometimes the spaces left by fire have not been filled by trees

for some reason not filled by trees. The spaces make attractive sunny glades.

The way to stay oriented in this vast wood, I find, is to keep track of the edge so, at the southwest end of the wood, we turn right, heading north, with the wood on our right. This is a short stretch and we soon come to the northwest corner where we again turn right to keep the wood on our right and the boundary on the left. We are now heading east.

The girth
and shapes
of mediaeval
hornbeam boles
are thrilling

And here, all along the north edge of the wood, we have a feast of mediaeval hornbeams, distorted from being laid into a boundary hedge. The shapes, the girths, the twists and turns, the markings on the bark of these trees are amazing – and there are hundreds of them one after the other lining our path

Some stems are
horizontal from
having been laid

that might once have been an ancient lane, golden underfoot in the autumn, lined with leafy green light in the summer.

Lane along the
north edge of
the wood

Paul Arnold with his grandson enjoying squirrel telly in an ancient long-ago-laid hornbeam

Here is a lane to linger in, appreciating the weird wood shapes and textures, noting the different species: mostly hornbeam (see the distinctive vertical lines on its bark), occasionally ash (a pale bark with diamond patterned grooves) or hazel (ultra-smooth bark and almost-vertical, more-slender shoots) and even field maple (miniature maple leaves, crusty bark).

On our right, a good way along, the trees change from being conifer mixed with other species to being the second section of the wood: the conifer plantation undamaged by fire. Here we see the uniformity of the planting: strict row after row. First the area was clear felled and the timber sold for

The middle section of the wood: foresters planted the trees in strict rows and to a pattern

the reconstruction work so needed after the war. Grants and tax advantages were available to give land owners the incentive to provide the nation with what was required at the time – and foreseen to be required in decades to come. Paul Arnold worked in forestry in the early 1950s and tells how he was employed in just such planting – in Shenley, for example. The pattern is of seven trees repeated over and over again to the end of the row: oak, oak, pine, pine, beech, pine pine; each two paces apart along a straight row. On he went for a day's work of planting a thousand trees: oak, pace, pace, oak, pace, pace, pine, pace, pace... The Gorhambury estate must have employed just such a team to do just such a job. The idea was that, if the planting had been done evenly, there would be groups of four oaks and pairs of beech trees from adjacent rows. The plan was that the pine would be extracted earlier than the broadleafs leaving the standard oaks and beeches to grow to their maturity. But it did not work out like that. We can see that it is only on the edge that a few oaks survived. I can see no beech and oak as I peer into the depths of the plantation. The rows of pines are there but the oaks and beeches are missing from them. Also, twenty years on, the market had changed and the pine timber was not worth the extraction costs. So here we are with most of the pines that were originally planted.

More abruptly, we come to the third section of the wood: the ancient woodland, managed over the millennia since Neolithic times. Coppiced hornbeam is predominant, last coppiced decades ago so that the 'new' growth is way above our heads. As would have been the practice through ancient

The third section of the wood is ancient woodland, mostly coppiced hornbeam and standard oaks

THE REMARKABLE TREES OF ST ALBANS REVISITED

times, standard oaks have been left to reach maturity(19) in amongst the coppiced hornbeam. We can turn in amongst the trees if we keep an eye on our direction and know where the edge of the wood is, but it is a good idea to return to the north edge to keep oriented. We find the occasional coppiced ash, a tall cherry or two (one has three branches like the prongs of a trident), clumps of birches and, near the edge where the light is strong, all sorts of young growth.

As we traverse the northern edge of the wood, we come across a beam of wood set into the earth(20). This was put in place to stem the torrents of water that flow off the fields and down a watercourse through the woods. By the beam, there is a cherry tree of amazing girth and height. I was astounded to see that this ancient tree still bears fruit. We can continue skirting the woods or follow the watercourse back, taking the left-hand path when we come to a grassy triangle and going right when we come to the southern side.

Oak with burrs

Shortly before we come to the south side of the wood, we see an oak covered in huge burrs (encrustations) from top to toe. It looks obese. There is a species of oak called a burr oak, *Quercus macrocarpa*, a native of America, but its leaves are on petioles (stalks) of 3–5 cm, which is not the case for this oak.

The golf course can be seen on our left through the trees, all sorts of them flourishing in the light. I walked this way with Donato Cinicolo who took the photographs (the good ones) for this book, and we paused where there is a cherry log lying on the ground. The log is a whopper. It comes up to my thigh.

Donato Cinicolo on a whopping cherry log

Look out for a very odd ash tree: the top of it has died but is still hanging in there whilst new branches have forked out round it. The bark on the new branches is so different from that of the main stem that the branches look as if they are a different species of tree.

As we come level with the central plantation, the path is somewhat wider and firmer than before and we are on what was made as a track along which to extract the timber. It has not yet been made use of.

When we are opposite the high netting(21) where we know it is relatively safe to cross the golf course, we retrace our steps to the car park.

There is much more to discover in each part of Batchwood, in different seasons, at different times of day, in different weather, in ones different moods, with ever increasing awareness. We are fortunate to have such a source of refreshment in St Albans.

Track created to extract timber

Speaking of refreshment, we can usually get at least a cup of tea in the Sports centre.

Sycamore across the fairway from the Sports Centre

Batchwood revisited

(1) The Friends of Batchwood arranged for the old ash tree in the woodland at the top of the drive into Batchwood to 'have its top taken off'. It is surviving and its pruning back has opened up the canopy to let in light. We can still see it beyond the red-disk 'no entry' sign as we emerge from the car park.

It is this exit from the car park that is the start of the described walking route through the woodlands of Batchwood. See the map.

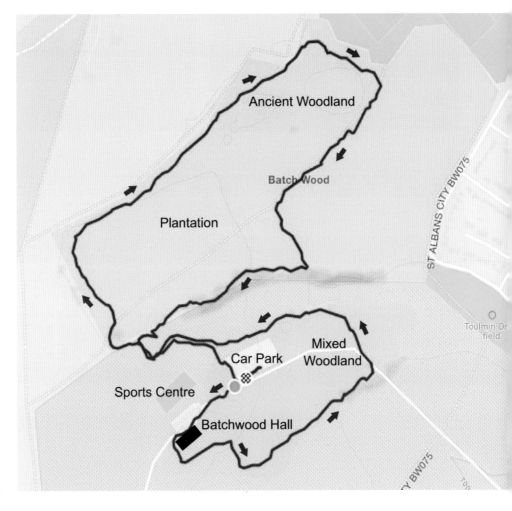

Batchwood
showing
walking route

(2) Although I was concerned in 2010 for beech trees too close to the path alongside Batchwood Hall, as at 2018, they are thriving.

(3) I called the boards on the small building by Batchwood putting green 'slabs' because they are remarkably wide and thick. However, I have been told that I ought to have described them as 'thick elm weatherboarding'. As at 2018, the hut is still there, looking forlorn with its door and windows boarded up.

A hut by the putting green at Batchwood with elm weatherboarding

(4) The broad path leading into mixed woodland that we turn left on to on our walking route is at the end of the terrace in front of Batchwood Hall.

(5) The work done by the Friends of Batchwood is to be applauded. It is remarkable that we have mixed woodland – now deemed to be 'ancient woodland' – within a kilometre of the City. The Friends do excellent work looking after it for us. Do join. The fees are £5 a year – and they have the best bring-and-share Summer picnic ever.

Also, it is healthier than going to the gym to help outdoors coppicing; fixing bat boxes and bird boxes; opening up canopies to give good vistas and more light; and creating informal hedging. The last is done by pushing over and holding down lines of oak and hazel where it is important to deter people from pushing through on to vulnerable ground where there are, for example, precious species of toothwort or wild narcissus.

Wild flowers tend not to like soils rich in nitrogen, but nettles and brambles do. The Friends of Batchwood try to confine the golf course green keepers' nitrogen-rich grass cuttings to specific dumping points.

(6) The short path up to the Friends of Batchwood picnic area is on the left up a little slope almost immediately after we turn on to the path into mixed woodland.

The biofuel willow can be identified at the entrance to the picnic area by its very narrow leaves. It is overshadowed by bigger trees but is hanging on in there.

(7) The humane squirrel traps, despite being placed high in the trees at Batchwood, kept getting removed by unknown persons. The Friends of Batchwood have given up on squirrel traps.

(8) It is easy to miss the rustic bench at the base of the oak tree that marks the path to Beryl Carrington's pretty rowan tree. See 'Trees with history revisited' for a photograph of it.

Close to Beryl's rowan you will see an alder. It was planted in memory of the father of one of the Friends of Batchwood.

(9) Beech wood left outdoors in Britain rots more quickly than some other woods. There is not much trace of the massive tree that fell, narrowly missing Beryl Carrington's rowan. In case you missed it, here is a photograph of the lurid fungi that grew along the length of the log.

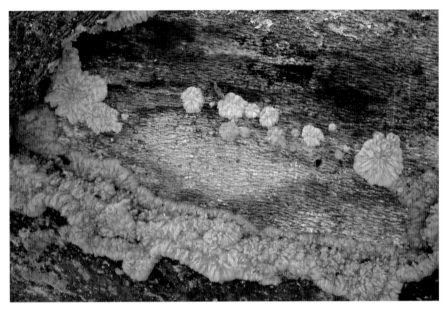

Fungi that were growing in 2010 on a fallen beech log in Batchwood

(10) We no longer need to leave our path to see the coppicing work done by the Friends of Batchwood. A great deal of it has been done over the years and we can see the varying design of baskets they have used.

(11) Nor do we need to leave the path to see – and feel the rough leaves of – elm trees. Several overhang the path after we have crossed the drive.

(12) At the height of Summer, it is difficult to see the very old beech tree from the path we are on. If at the T-junction of paths we turn right, uphill, for a short way, we can see the tree, now on our right, more easily.

(13) The scientific name for Turkey oaks is *Quercus cerris*.

(14) The scientific name for field maples is *Acer campestre*.

(15) It is less easy to see on Google Earth the distinction between the conifer plantation damaged by fire and the rest of the plantation. The glades left by fire damage have been filled in – and by a wider range of species of tree.

The distinction between plantation and ancient woodland, however, is clear, both on Google Earth and in reality.

(16) The typical crown of our native small-leafed lime, *Tilia cordata*, is tall with an irregular dense dome formed by arching branches.

Our other native lime, the large-leafed lime, *Tilia platyphyllos*, is taller and narrow.

The common lime, *Tilia x europaea*, is a hybrid of our two natives, and tends to pick up its shape-genes from the latter: it too is tall and narrow.

Got that? Small-leafed lime has wide, arching branches; others are tall and narrow.

Do you remember the other signifier of the small leafed lime? Its flowers stick out in every direction rather than being pendulous.

Lime trees were the commonest tree in lowland England during the warm Atlantic period, 7–5000 years ago (Rackham, 2006, p.84). The sharp decline in numbers of lime trees at the end of the Atlantic period was in some part due to their inability to set viable seed in the cooler climate of the following millennia. But now with recent climate warming in Britain, native limes are again beginning to set viable seed. They are the positive image of global warming (Miles, 2006, pp.26–27).

Here, on our path we have a veteran small leafed lime. Its boughs arch out and its trunk is gloriously patterned, gnarled and grooved.

Close to it, towards the house, are two European limes, distinctively tall and narrow. We can compare the shapes that distinguish them.

The typical arching bough of a small leafed lime

(17) The gap at the end of the netting has been blocked off so that we need to go to the end of the trees in line with the netting before we can turn right and cross the fairway behind the tee into the woods.

(18) From the map of our walking route through Batchwood, we can see that the plantations and ancient woodland are set at an angle so that, throughout, it would be more accurate to say that rather than heading west, north, east and then south, we head southwest, then northwest, northeast, southeast, southwest, southeast again and, finally, southwest back to the car park.

Also, it is more accurate to say that the distorted mediaeval hornbeams are along the northwest edge of the woods.

(19) It has been suggested to me that standard oaks would have been left to grow only to a size of trunk that the then-current tools could deal with, perhaps the diameter of a hand's span. However, I have also been told that Neolithic tools were remarkably efficient and could have coped with felling huge trunks. 'Probably' is a useful word. We may never know the reality, but it is life-enhancing, I find, to consider the possibilities and decide on probabilities when walking through ancient woodland.

Take the right
ork at an island
n the path and,
vhere there are
wo logs and a
beam set into the
earth, turn right
and follow
. watercourse

(20) Retracing the steps of the described walking route, I kept wondering why I had not reached the 'beam of wood set into the earth' that marks the turning point. I found myself with only the field ahead. The key thing is to keep right where there is an island in the path. See the photo. Curve right and keep going until you do come to the beam of wood set into the earth on the path. On the left is a pair of giant logs marking a path into the field. Turn your back on beam and logs and head down the watercourse.

The beam and logs will always be there, I think, but the adjacent 'cherry tree of amazing girth' may not be for much longer. Ominously, it has the number 88 spray-painted on it. I assume that means it is for the chop.

I did not see the oak with burrs, the whopping cherry log or the odd-looking ash tree described but there is a massive beech early on and lots of wonderful or weird or homely trees to enjoy on the walk back.

It looks as if the cherry tree of amazing girth is destined for the chop

(21) It is easy to walk past the path we want to take us back across the fairway. Look for a sycamore with three stems and a sawn-off branch and follow the lady on the left, to be seen in the photograph.

The path out of the woods is marked by a 3-stemmed sycamore

Harpenden and Rothamsted

Would it be going too far to say that it is the trees that make Harpenden so visually attractive? The town's architecture is pleasingly mellow but its trees are beautiful.

Ask Harpenden residents about their trees and the one that first comes to mind is almost invariably the ancient horsechestnut that is the first tree to come into leaf. It is on the corner of the High Street and Station Road and is included in 'Our favourite trees'. Then the 'baa lamb' trees are mentioned. This is a handsome group of trees opposite The Silver Cup on the main road in from St Albans. No one is sure why they are called this, and I suspect that both the name and its uncertain origin(1) are part of the appeal.

Copper beech,
Harpenden Hall

The wonderful willows by the Lea in Batford get mentioned. They are chocolate-box perfect in their setting by the iron bridge. The huge poplars there and along the river are terrific: a little ford at the end of Crabtree Lane is as idyllic as it gets – and it is the surrounding trees that make it so.

What is surprising is that no one bothers to mention the superb copper beech at Harpenden Hall, Southdown Road. To anyone coming into Harpenden on St Albans Road, this is a most eye-catching tree, partly for its size, partly for its colour and partly for its position across the Common.

Residents seem also to take for granted the splendid row of green and copper beeches(2) between Leyton Road (the one in front of the fire station by The Silver Cup) and St Albans Road, and do not bother to mention the array of horsechestnuts and medley of other broadleafs along the High Street in front of the shops.

My personal favourite is a tall tree in Leyton Green. It has a tapering shape and delightfully dainty foliage. It is a dawn redwood, *Metasequoia glyptostroboides*.

Dawn redwood in Leyton Green

Another dainty tree of great beauty is a scarlet oak, *Quercus coccinnea*, planted by the Royal Agricultural Society to mark 150 years of experiments at Rothamsted. As you enter the research station at the main gate, the scarlet oak is on the corner in front of the pleasing red brick building on the right. Its leaves in autumn are bright scarlet and then gradually turn deep wine red, the lower branches holding onto their leaves, by then dark red-brown, well into the late autumn. Alan Mitchell describes the scarlet oak as 'wispy'. It will never reach the great stature we associate with mature English oaks but that teaches us to value the variety in tree form (Mitchell 1976).

In Harpenden, ordinary places have lovely trees, some of them specimen trees. It is not uncommon, as we drive along the residential roads looking for an address, to find we are passing a white-barked tree or giant sequoia right on the verge; there is a splendid oak in the top corner of Lydekker car park off Sun Lane; there is a charming group of horsechestnuts in the green at the centre of Springfield Crescent.

White-barked tree on a residential street

There is a horsechestnut(3) on Grove Road that is a focus in the streetscape and, what I particularly like about it, is that kids climb it. The tree is on the edge of a purpose-built playground and it is as if the tree is an extension of the playground.

Robert Naylor-Stables

A host of tall conifers points heavenwards as we enter the Westfield Road cemetery, a pair of giant sequoias teaches us how insignificant we are, and the great copper beeches and other beautiful trees remind us how wonderful it is to be alive.

Hatching Green is on Redbourn Lane, not far from the intersection with St Albans Road. It is a proper green, a triangular open grassed area. At the top of it is a caricature of a beech tree; a caricature in that one of its branches strikes upwards and outwards at an acute angle, others at right angles, as beech branches do but usually less obviously. Once we have seen it, it helps us to recognise a beech tree in winter by its branch pattern. Next to it is a fountaining birch and then some horsechestnuts. Along the road edge are a hornbeam, a copper beech, a lime, a walnut and a mountain ash, each a first-rate example of its species.

If we cross the golf course on East Common from St Albans Road by way of Limbrick Road, we find we are passing through oak woods which, according to the information board on the Common by The Three Horseshoes, are self-seeded. The oak tree shapes are not what we expect: they are more twisting and spreading, branching lower than we are used to from hedgerow, garden or pastureland oaks.

And then we come to an amazing pair of three-needled pines. Their great trunks curve and coil outwards towards us and then up and up, great cones starting from the trunk itself, long clusters of needles forming their foliage. These are in the grounds of Limbrick Hall and behind them is what can only be called a crowd of Victorian trophy trees: a couple of giant sequoias, a true cedar almost as tall as the sequoias, and a throng of Western red cedars and Lawson cypresses. East Common ends Limbrick Road and, as we look along it to the right towards Grange Court Road, we see more and more colossal conifers. This is a remarkable corner of Harpenden.

Rothamsted Park

The avenue of limes(4) is the first thing we encounter as we enter Rothamsted Park from the gates near the fire station in Leyton Road. The land slopes down and then up and away, heightening the effect of being led onwards.

There is a small formal park to our left, a picture of deep-pink blossom in spring, and there is parkland beyond on either side of the avenue.

Avenue of limes, Rothamsted Park

A park within Rothamsted Park

At the top of the hill, we can take a path that forks to the right alongside the national willow collection. It is interesting to see the different textures, densities and heights of the growth, and to read the information board explaining how we are trying to find the best varieties for drought conditions, for wet conditions, for pest resistance and so on, and to find out about the wildlife the willows live with.

We are within the grounds of Rothamsted Research now and information boards tell us about the work being done and also provide maps showing rights of way and permissive paths that take us round the Manor.

Rothamsted Manor

There is a very pretty avenue of low-arching cherry trees taking us in towards Rothamsted Manor and, at the far side of the pond on the left by the low ornamental brick wall as we come on to the drive in front of the house, a great beast of an oak. It has a girth of 550cm – five and a half metres – and an amazingly textured trunk.

The two glossy leaved trees against the wall at either end of the house are *Magnolia grandiflora*, so named for the size of their heavily lemon-scented flowers, and the climbing plant close to the one on the right is a kiwi fruit.

Further along the drive is a ring of towering lime trees. There was probably a lime a generation older in the centre and these are shoots from it that have been allowed – encouraged perhaps – to grow to replace their progenitor now long gone.

A black walnut, *Juglans nigra*, has been planted close to the drive as it bends towards the house and, in amongst the bank of tall trees behind it, is an Asiatic elm(5), *Ulmus pumila*. It has not so far been infected with Dutch elm disease. It will never be a spectacular tree but it is interesting to see another species of elm.

An old oak by the pond near the Manor house

Magnolia grandiflora flowers intermittently through all seasons

We are permitted to walk along the drive but, to go along the side of the Manor House, we have to wait until there is a Rothamsted Research open day, which I could not more highly recommend. There are graphic and tangible displays of fascinating information. Even from the drive we can see the magnificent pair of copper beech trees, one even older than the other and (on an open day), if we go across and behind them, we are in a space bounded on either side by the tallest imaginable trees. Our eyes are drawn to an extraordinary statue that is the reason for, and deliberate focal point of, our shaped space. It is a wild and wonderful sculpture, thrilling and frighteningly full of action

and energy. The woman being tied to the back of the frenzied bull is Dirce. She had tried to kill the mother of the two strong men, who are pinioning her down with ropes. We can see their names carved in Greek, Zethus and Amphion, and that of the sculptor carved in English, Charles Bennet Lawes-Wittewronge, one of the members of the family who owned the Rothamsted estate.

Behind the statue rise giant sequoias. Does their calm immobility enhance our awe?

The walk back from the sculpture towards the Manor is made superb by our glorious copper beech trees.

Returning to the drive and continuing on, we come to a row of venerable lime trees, hemlocks, yews, a coastal redwood and the giant sequoias that back the sculpture. There are impressively tall trees along the path that takes us steadily round to the far side of the house.

Giant sequoias make a fitting backdrop to an extraordinary sculpture

Across to the west on the far side of the fields is Knott Wood which, despite having been clear felled in 1937, is designated ancient woodland. This is because there are unambiguous records of it having been managed woodland for 400 years. Oak and beech were planted in the 1940s and it is interesting to see how many more of them have survived than those planted in amongst the pines in Batchwood. There is a path along the edge of Knott Wood and between the path and the adjacent

Copper beech
at Rothamsted
Manor

field there is a line of ash trees. It is such a definite line that I thought they
had been deliberately planted as a hedge. A first! An ash hedge! But, no,
the trees are self seeded. Next time I passed I was amazed to see that the ash
trees had been laid. I should not have been surprised to find that it was the
photographer for this book, Donato Cinicolo, assisted by his wife Rosie, who
had laid them.

Harpenden and Rothamsted revisited

(1) I thought the origin of 'Baa Lamb trees' had to do with the sheep that grazed
on Harpenden Common and, while helping with a Heartwood visitor survey,
I met a man who told me that his great grandfather had been a shepherd on
Harpenden Common. That seemed to confirm it: we can imagine grownups
pointing out the 'baa lambs' to tots until the name 'baa lamb' stuck.

However, through wills, maps and interesting rings of scorched grass that
appeared in the drought of 1976 and could be matched to old maps, it seems
that a house called 'Balams' stood from at least 1652 until at least the middle
of the 18th century where the Baa Lamb trees are now (Freeman, 1977).

We also find that the various owners of this property also had farmland
that included land where Bylands House is now on the old A5 about half a

mile north of Redbourn. The supposition is that the owners built and moved to the house on their farm, and the original house and its outbuildings on Harpenden Common were demolished (ibid.).

I delight in the evolution of the of the name as it appears in will and maps from Balams, through Balambs, Bailams, Bear Lambs to our present day Baa Lambs and Bylands – and they might be 'an altered form of the personal name 'Balaam' (ibid.).

Baa Lamb trees, Harpenden Common

(2) The row of alternating green and copper beeches along Leyton Road in Harpenden were planted to replace a row of English elms devastated by Dutch Elm Disease in the 1970s. They were one of the last lots of English elms to succumb to the disease. Paul Arnold put their resistance down to the protection of street pollution covering their bark.

(3) There is a venerable horsechestnut on the verge by the playground on Grove Road, Southdown, Harpenden. It is outside the fence round the playground so might not be the tree that Robert Naylor-Stables liked for being climbed by children as part of the purpose-built playground. The first branches off the trunk are a good two metres above the ground so that children would need a good hoik up but, once up, there are good thick branches to snuggle into – and I hope children do.

A horsechestnut tree is an extension of the playground in Grove Road, Harpenden

(4) I like to read of Edwin Grey's use of the term 'carriage way' in its original sense, 'a way for carriages'. Writing in 1922 of what must be the avenue past the Sports Centre into Rothamsted Park, he tells us, 'The carriage way to the village that is now, was made, and the lime trees on either side planted somewhat over 40 years ago' (Grey, 1922). That means that the trees were planted in 1882 or earlier, making them more than 130 years old

(5) Elms have leaves that are markedly rough to the touch. Use this useful tree-identity check on the Asiatic elm at the entrance to Rothamsted Manor.

Frank Britain, County Scout historian, put me in touch with Ray Vassie who helps the Scouts with his knowledge of trees in Rothamsted. Ray tells us of a whitebeam sapling that fell in the storm of 1987.

'The park keepers were busy managing the big trees that fell,' Ray tells us, 'And the small horizontal whitebeam was overlooked. The trunk stayed on the grass, but growth resumed its upward path. You can see it if you look ahead when you get to the end of the lime avenue coming from Rothamsted Park. It's not impressive but is a curio.' An indomitable whitebeam!

Also in Rothamsted Park, is an oak planted by Sir John Lawes in 1887 to commemorate the golden jubilee of Queen Victoria. It is not far from the mobile-phone mast near the football club. It has a plaque next to it.

CHAPTER EIGHT

Villages, woodlands and the countryside

Wheathampstead(1)

As we come down Brewhouse Hill into Wheathampstead, we see the soaring spire of St Helens church ahead backed by a distant bank of trees of every texture and shade. As we descend, the closer trees take the view and our eye is drawn to a golden robinia in a garden in the foreground on the right, and then to a great floppy walnut(2) on the left with the zigzag brick-in-flint of the old school beyond it. And now we are abreast of St Helens: a cherry on the pavement, picturesque with blossom in the spring and with crimson leaves in the autumn; a tall larch, bright green in spring, dark green in summer, dripping

Corsican pines at the top of Ash Grove in Wheathampstead

in cones all year; an even taller towering lime; and an over-arching magnificent wing nut, *Pterocarya fraxinifolia*. At first, I mistook the wing nut for a walnut because both have big rich-green compound leaves and early soon-shed male catkins, but there is no mistaking the female catkins of the wing nut. They are pendulous, pink and as long as an adult hand, elongating to twice that length and strung with circular winged green fruit in summer. After the wing nut are a couple of Irish yews and some Western

Caucasian wingnut

red cedars and then an Indian bean tree, which is one of a pair. Wow! What an entrance!

We might be tempted to turn in alongside the old school to have a closer look at St Helens. If so, we would be in Bury Green and we would immediately see at the top of the hill ahead a group of exceptionally large pine trees. These are Corsican pines and one of them has a girth of more than a metre. If we are tempted to take a closer look, our climb up the hill will be rewarded by the majesty of these conifers. If we follow their line and continue down Ash Grove, at the bottom of the hill we come to an ash tree(3) that is pure joy to look at. While I watched, I saw tiny tits at the very tips of the twigs starting about

One of a pair of American Indian bean trees flanked by Irish yews in St Helens churchyard

and changing places with their mates, darting off as a pair of magpies jumped closer and closer, too heavy to get to them: but the tits took no chances. The tree has a lovely spreading shape from a stately stem.

We can curl round along Ash Grove until we find ourselves in Canons Field, an open recreation space, where there are lovely spreading cedars and a huge red oak(4) right next to the children's play area. It has bracket fungus so we need to savour its grandeur while we can. See how its branches reach out and twist upwards. Find its small button-like acorns with their patterned cups. Note its large leaves and proper petioles(5).

A path leads us down into St Helens churchyard where there is another feast of trees.

Coming into Wheathampstead along the Marford Road are attractive old and young cherry trees and whitebeams. Along the river, are huge poplars and willows: everywhere trees adding to the beauty of the village of Wheathampstead.

Sandridge and Heartwood Forest(6)

I love the tall Scots pine on Sandridge High Street. It is in the grounds of Lyndon House, very close to the road behind a curved flint wall and a hedge. The top of the tree seems particularly tall against the sky and has a graceful shape.

Heartwood Forest is the name the Woodland Trust has given to the vast area it is now responsible for in Sandridge. It is to be the largest new native forest in England. 600,000 trees will be planted and there will be wildflower meadows, orchards, vistas and rides.

Heartwood includes the ancient Langley Wood where St Albans people go to see bluebells in spring. It is a magical wood. Just thinking about being within it makes any tension roll from the shoulders. It has been managed in the past as a hornbeam-coppice and oak-standard wood and there are parts of it that have been coppiced more recently than others, encouraging biodiversity. Along the south-western side of Langley Wood there are some attractive old lime trees, but they do not quite compare with the venerable

Scots pine,
Sandridge

spreading small leafed limes in Well Wood, which is bit further up the main path that comes up from the village and passes Langley Wood on the left and then Well Wood on the right. If we know what we are looking for, the limes can be seen as we approach Well Wood from Langley Wood. They are not of the tall-thin variety but have round crowns. Even within the wood they are not easy to get to because the undergrowth is dense and the paths within the wood do not go particularly close to them. However, if we take the path that skirts the wood on the Sandridge side, we can see them clearly.

The Woodland Trust is hoping that paths through these woods will develop naturally as we find our way through them. There is good access now and we can walk through any time, but it is worth attending the bluebell and summer festivals, planting trees and joining working parties in Heartwood. We can link up with super people in welcoming helpful volunteer groups, sign up for newsletters and make donations to help with the work that needs to be done. The obvious starting place is www.woodlandtrust.org.uk or call 0845 293 5706 for local organisers.

Bricket Wood(7)

Bricket Wood Common is as ancient as woodland gets and has been designated a Site of Special Scientific Interest (SSSI). How dark and weird it seems as we turn into School Lane and find ourselves in a tunnel of trees with almost no undergrowth beneath them. Further on it opens out and, although the trees are still predominantly hornbeam, it seems lighter and there is more undergrowth. Further on there is a section that was clear-felled to re-create some of the heathland that was more extensive here a century ago when Commoners exercised their grazing rights. Trouble was taken to protect newts and other pond life but the contractors' equipment made deep ruts that filled with and held water, making the place a quagmire for ages. Silver birches have colonised some parts of the area, others have been kept clear as heathland, and there are

Hornbeam and standard oak at Bricket Wood Common

plans to bring back grazing. One of the reasons the site was given SSSI status was that wet acidic heathland, which is what we have here, is rare. The area has also been designated a High Biodiversity Area and St Albans District Council, the Countryside Management Service, DEFRA and Capel Manor College are all working together to undertake projects to optimise biodiversity. There are plans for more information boards, so watch this space.

Acidic wet heathland within Bricket Wood Common

The lessons of damage by heavy equipment in Bricket Wood Common were learned and, when it came to working in Blackgreen Wood, which is north of Bricket Wood Common off Lye Lane, horses were used to extract felled timber. The plan is to tackle a fifth of the wood each year for the next five years: coppicing and felling and undergrowth clearing. There is a lot of work to be done here, and the Council also has Nottlers Wood and Mutchetts Wood to look after.

Hanstead Wood in the grounds of the HSBC Training College(8) is being capably looked after by the Friends of Hanstead Wood, and they have received a Green Pennant Award for the work they have been doing, planting native trees, putting up bird and bat boxes, creating a small delightful wildflower meadow and creating picnic facilities. Anyone can visit and be welcome. Turn into the training college (signed on Smug Oak Lane), turn into the car park, and you will see the entrance to Hanstead Wood. Within the wood was a tree nursery for the stately home that the college building used to be and there are lines of trees about a metre apart, tall and thin and straight, presumably planted as seedlings and never planted out. The specimen trees that *were* planted out in the parkland can be seen as we come into the site.

The Friends of Hanstead Wood meet to do what needs to be done on the second Saturday of the month and would welcome volunteers. They even have their own website: www.hansteadwood.co.uk.

London Colney

Willows, silver birches, a great horsechestnut and a neat rowan turn the space on either side of the High Street bridge over the Colne into an idyllic spot for picnickers, children fishing for water-life and imbibers at The Green Dragon. On one side, the silver birches make an inviting glade tempting us to a riverside walk. On the other side, a footbridge beckons us to the tree-lined lakes made from old gravel pits.

Trees make an idyll of the river bank by The Green Dragon

The Colney Fox has soaring broadleafs and conifers behind it and the High Street has lines of alternating maples and the odd lone pine to soften the scene and lift our eyes from the road.

And then there is Napsbury Park.

Napsbury Hospital was founded in 1898 and was an asylum for all but a few years of the whole of the 20th century and a military hospital in the First World War. William Golding designed the grounds and Napsbury is thought to be the only complete surviving instance of his many prestigious landscape designs. Golding's designs are informal and at Napsbury he took care to preserve existing trees, which accounts for the wonderfully mature native trees as well as a staggering collection of the specimen trees Victorians delighted in.

Broadleaf trees behind The Colney Fox

I thought I knew what to expect of Napsbury. Victorian rectors competed to have the best specimen trees and we have Hill End Hospital grounds and Cell Barnes so we know to expect cedars and sequoias and so on. But Napsbury has the real wow factor. Yes, right from our entrance, there are grand horsechestnuts, red ones in the central reservation, a good copper beech, a golden ash, cedars of Lebanon, deodar cedars, Atlantic cedars (blue and green). It is all magnificent and wonderful. What is exceptional is the scale of the planting. There are whole groups of magnificent trees.

As we go up a side road within the estate we see a whole line of Atlantic cedars stretching out into the countryside carrying our eyes to the water tower at Napsbury's sister asylum away over at Shenley. Beyond it is a shimmering great poplar backed by a line of Lombardy poplars and broadleafs and conifers away to a huge old comfortably spreading tree.

Closer in, across a lawn from the converted asylum buildings, is the hugest hornbeam I have ever seen, its branches dripping with its distinctive clusters of golden three-winged seeds. And what can that great spreading tree be? Amazingly, it is a wild cherry, its trunk the

Hornbeam seeds

An ancient cherry tree

girth of an old beech. Speaking of which, there are several of them – huge beings – and an ash, and a Lawson cypress or six.

Close to the water tower is a dawn redwood. It is darker green than the one in Harpenden's Leyton Green and probably twice its age. You should be lucky enough to see the cones. They are nearer spherical than cones usually are, a bit bigger than a hazel nut, not as big as a walnut, grooved horizontally, green in September, dangling on a stalk. Can you see the tiny pointed growths on the underside of some of the leaves at the base of the

Dawn redwood cones

leaflets? This is distinctive of the dawn redwood. They are leaf buds. See how floppy the growth is at the end of the branches and how much more strongly the leaves above twist and flare. As the autumn progresses the leaves will turn pink and then red and finally fall. Yes, it is a conifer, a deciduous conifer – as is the larch.

Further on, across a line of mature wild cherries and an asphalt path, is a tall turkey oak. See how narrow the leaves are and that they are each on a stalk, unlike our English oak, and the plates on its bark are as wide as my hand. Turkey oak acorns take two years to develop and our tree had few acorns in 2010, but I was able to find one or two, not completely formed but with the very distinctive cup covered in curls that curl upwards on the upside and downwards on the downside. A bracket fungus is evident at the base of the turkey oak, and part of its bark has been torn away. This latter wound

Bracket fungus at the base of a turkey oak

is very sad, but it is nevertheless interesting to see the depth of the outer bark crust: it must be 12cm thick. Behind it is an English oak. It better beware the knopper gall wasp that will love it here with generation after generation of wasps alternating within their life cycles between the handy English and Turkey oaks.

On a happier note, also close to the turkey oak is a bird cherry(9), one of our undisputed 33 native trees. See its spherical black berries and buddleia-shaped blossom in spring.

Tucked behind a house at the edge of the parkland is a five-needle pine. It has whiskery needles and abundant cones narrow but longer than the length of my hand. They drip picturesque droplets of clear resin when they are green.

As we look through to the parkland we see spreading oaks and beech trees, glimpse a crimson king maple and note the spiky conifers.

Clear resin dripping down the cone of a five-needle pine

Along another drive there is a whole group of three-needle pines, Corsican pines I would say. Because they are so grouped they are spectacular: an array of silver-patterned trunks beneath, a riot of bristly foliage above. Behind is the

Corsican pines

kind of bank of trees we are more used to: soft blue-green birch, spreading brighter beech, pointed pines, feathery ash. Elsewhere there are masses of purple prunus, a rich burgundy in summer and glorious with blossom in spring.

Napsbury is an exceptionally lovely park to have within the District.

Redbourn(10)

Avenue of limes across Redbourn Common

Coming towards Redbourn from St Albans we see a group of Lombardy poplars on the left, and then a group of huge glossy lively spreading poplars immediately before the filling station. Less than a hundred yards further on, at the roundabout(11) entrance to the village itself, there are more poplars and willows. The village is at the confluence of the rivers Ver and Red, hence the water-loving poplars and willows.

Redbourn is on Watling Street, the Roman road straight as a die from Marble Arch to Holyhead. For millennia, travelers have paused here for refreshment and supplies. In the middle ages, pilgrims, tradesmen and craftsmen came to the priory; in the 18th century well-to-do families built substantial houses and planted prestigious trees; and trees in private gardens and public spaces have been planted and tended up to the present day. As I gaze out of the window while I am strengthening and lengthening my back during Pilates classes in the top-floor Guide room of the village hall, I see trees of every different hue and texture, shape and size.

There is a public garden through the great green double gates on the High Street. At first we are in a short avenue of English yew trees, some female with bright red fruits, some male without. Our heads are drawn back to follow upwards the height of a giant sequoia on the far side of the wall. There are lovely new trees in the garden and dark Irish yews. If we go through the arched gate and go left, we come out onto the Common. In the autumn there is a carpet of gold and deep red at our feet from the

New trees and yew trees

fallen leaves of a grove of mature maples, and ahead of us is wide open space with an avenue of limes stretching across the Common towards Church End. There is a cedar next to the old school away to our left (south) and beyond that a playground set about with cherry trees. By the river are mature weeping willows and poplars.

Trees round Redbourn Common

THE REMARKABLE TREES OF ST ALBANS REVISITED

At the end of the footpath under the avenue of limes is Church End which takes us into St Marys churchyard. A line of limes points to the ancient cedar of Lebanon and an avenue of ancient pollarded limes leads to the church. In 2010 every resident contributed in one way or another to celebrate the 900th anniversary of the founding of the church.

Pollarded limes within St Marys churchyard

Childwickbury

On the way to Harpenden from St Albans is Childwickbury. The best way to go is to walk from Batchwood, through the fruit farm, onto Harpenden Road and then turn in through the mammoth towers of alternating layers of red and yellow brick that mark the entrance to Childwickbury. The drive is lined

with rhododendrons and azaleas and behind them are superb oak and ash and sweet chestnut trees. We come to the understated red brick church of St Mary with the beautiful copper beech arching over it (see Our Favourites). We can veer left (south east) and walk on through Childwickbury Green and the Childwickbury Estate

The drive into Childwickbury

back to Batchwood and on our way we shall see a lovely oak wood, two rare trees and wonderful views.

The oak wood is on our left soon after we pass the lodge. It is a picture in spring with bluebells spread beneath the trees.

One tree is not an oak. It is a manna ash, *Fraxinus ornus*, and it originates in south eastern Europe. It is close to the hedge at the far end of the wood. Working back from the hedge, there is an ash, an alder (oval cone-like seeds on the tree all year round) and a lime, and the manna ash is between the alder and the lime, set back from the railings that edge our track. The common ash is wind pollinated but the

Opposite:
Rare European
white elm in
Childwickbury

Right: The
manna ash

manna ash has flowers with petals and scent to attract insects. I have only seen pictures of the flowers but they show bright pink stamens and white petals that are an inch long and only a small fraction of an inch wide. The petals radiate outwards in every direction and are arranged very close together making a long spiky cylindrical shape. We are told that the flowers come out at the same time as the leaves so we need to visit our tree in the spring.

The manna ash is a slow growing tree and is often grafted onto a common ash stock rather than being grown from seed. The bark is smooth and grey, quite different from the grooved beige bark of the common ash. The leaves are pinnate like those of the common ash but the foliage is much more dense. The seeds are single-winged like those of the common ash.

After the oak wood, there is open countryside on either side of our track, especially so on the right where we have views over fields and, further on, long views across the valley to the Gorhambury Estate. The land is mostly used as pasture and the trees have been cropped by grazing animals to a good 1.5 metres above the ground. It gives the trees the distinctive broad-based outline of countryside trees. See how the browsing has the same effect as a hedge trimmer: the leaves are more prolific and the foliage more dense along the browsing line.

There is also a rather odd pair of trees in the middle distance. I would say that the one on the right is an ash and is in poor health. It will be interesting to watch developments. Do you think the ash will collapse and the oak expand into the better light on that side? It is too late to hope that the oak will ever straighten up.

An odd couple of trees

We pass on our left the entrance to Childwickbury Manor and note the attractive yew, maple and prunus at the gate and tall conifers as we look towards the house and walk past the grounds behind.

Soon after a hump in the road and a bend to the right, we come to a lime and then a tree that is attractive but not noticeably unusual. It is, however, another rare tree, officially identified as a European white elm, *Ulmus laevis*. The photograph is looking back at it after we have passed it so that it is now on our left. The bark is in soft grey-beige strands, rather than the dark-grey finely grooved bark of the mature wych elm in Clarence Park.

If we retrace our steps back towards Childwickbury, we realise that we passed another elm tree on the same side as the European white elm about 100 metres back. There is yellow lichen on its bark and the branches spread from about two metres up. It has extraordinarily dense foliage. Feel how rough the leaves are, and hear how they rustle in our hand – as we would expect from an elm. The leaf edges are markedly serrated and each leaf is asymmetrical about the central vein but the leaf does

not quite go back to the stalk as do other elm leaves. It is difficult to say whether it is another European white elm, the trees being of such different maturity.

From here, we can yet again turn right round and head for Batchwood, or carry on back to Childwickbury.

European white elm

Another elm and detail of its leaves

The countryside

Oaks in a
Gorhambury field

Given its proximity to London, the countryside around St Albans is astonishingly rural. We have an enviable network of footpaths and they take us through woodland, alongside pasture for suckling herds or quagmires for pigs, across fields of wheat, barley, blue-flowered flax or yellow-flowered rape. Within the fields and pastures is often a lone oak or a line of oaks. Farm animals huddle under the trees to find shade or shelter from the rain. In arable fields, we can see how close the crops are planted to the trees and this means that farm equipment will drive over and dig over the roots. We are losing many trees this way. 'Set-aside', incentives to leave a meadow border round crops, gave hedge trees some respite but that scheme has been discontinued(12).

Along the lines of rivers we see poplars, especially huge on the banks of the River Lea at Batford, and also our native crack willow, white willow and goat willow.

The Tree Register and the Woodland Trust Ancient Tree Hunt log trees of great girth and I have been to find the ones in our District. On a popular circular walk from Redbourn to Redbournbury and back via the edge of Harpenden golf course, we pass an ash tree that is said to have a girth of 3 metres – exceptional for an ash which is not generally a long-lived tree. It can be seen close to Hammond End farmhouse along with some impressive pines and Western red cedars. Walking south from The Old Fox in Bricket Wood there is a whole avenue of gigantic beech trees with a girth nearing 4 metres. They are on the track leading over the M1.

But most huge wonderful trees in the countryside live their lives unrecorded, probably loved and hated in equal measure by landowners and farm workers, admired by us as we see them when we are out walking or travelling by car, bus or train through the countryside.

Hedges

Wherever we are in our District there are lines of hedges, remarkable miles of miniature woodland, home to dormice, voles and shrews and hedgehogs, home to birds, home to grubs and caterpillars and spiders and beetles,

September hedgerow fruits

home to foxes and badgers and rabbits. Hazel nuts, haws, sloes, blackberries, holly berries, rose hips and all sorts of seeds are in abundance for creatures, including bats, in autumn; catkins and blossom give nectar; leaves are food for caterpillars and grubs. The Tree Council claims that 600 plant species, 1,500 insect species, 65 bird and 20 mammal species have been recorded as living in hedges. If they are all living in the same space, an ecological balance is critical. It is best if the hedges can be corridors between woodlands so that the gene pool is kept healthily wide.

OPAL(13), the Open Air Laboratories Network that is linked to the Open University, wants to find out more about what is living in our hedges and from September to October 2010 asked as many people as possible to take part in a biodiversity survey by exploring their local hedges and recording what they found. Lots of us took part at Heartwood Forest. We await results.

There is reference in Caesar's 'Gallic Wars' to what scholars think are hedges, which must mean that rows of trees have been planted and cut for millennia. There was a network of hedges in Saxon times but it is the period from 1750 to 1850, as a result of the Enclosures Acts, that saw a massive increase in the number of hedges.

Left to themselves, hedges will shoot up. On the edge of a wood above Sandridge I was amazed to see 12 metre high blackthorn trees. They looked wispy and straggly – and it will be more difficult now to get them under control as part of a hedge. Left to themselves, hedges will also 'creep': the hedge trees will throw shoots from the base and drop fruits that take root close in where the plough does not reach them so that the hedge gradually gets wider and wider. Left to themselves, hedges will also get 'leggy': round the base of the tree there is no foliage in which small animals can hide.

Hedges are, therefore, not left to themselves. Sometimes they were coppiced and the cut branches layed on top of the stools so that new shoots would weave themselves through the branches. This was known as 'arable hedging' – 'arable' because it was firm enough to make a decent edging but would not be stock-proof. I noticed in September 2010 that along a hedge between Sandridge and Ayres End the hedge cuttings had been laid in piles alongside the hedge. The cuttings were long – many years' growth – and this must have been seen as the best way to tackle a difficult task.

Brash cuttings placed alongside a hedge

Best practice is laying(14) the hedge. A slice of the trunk is cut and bent back into a near-horizontal position. This slice is called a 'pleacher' and the slice needs to be thick enough to contain the sap-carrying vessels under the bark. The pleachers are held in their new position by an array of stakes woven together by flexible stems, usually hazel. The work is best done in autumn and early winter and, in the spring, the new growth can be spectacular: fresh and green and prolific, weaving itself through the lattice of stakes and adjacent pleachers. It is best to repeat(15) the work after about 15 or 20 years to keep the growth vigorous and the hedge dense to the base.

Hedge laying is a skilled job but we are fortunate in St Albans District in having skilled hedge layers. Donato Cinicolo, who took the photographs for this book, is an expert hedge layer, five times(16) (so far) the Hertfordshire champion. Wherever we went taking photographs, there seemed to be what I came to think of as one of Donato's friends: a hedge that he had laid. We are fortunate, too, that Hertfordshire hedge layers meet to exchange experience. One of their number is a man well into his eighties. He told the others that there is a Hertfordshire method of laying: instead of using only cut vertical stakes, where there is a suitable living upright, it can be lopped and incorporated as a stake. Growth will shoot from the base of this living stake, contributing to the density of the hedge. In 2010, for the first time, the county hedge-laying championship will use the Hertfordshire method instead of the former Midlands method(17).

Donato and the other hedge layers have been helping new people to perfect the craft. We are fortunate that people in our District understand the value in every conceivable way of keeping our hedges viable, and are taking the time to learn how to do so.

To keep hedge foliage dense, hedges need to be trimmed each year or every second year, even between laying. Trimming hedges is a big job and is invariably done these days by a mechanical cutter.

It was a tree warden that alerted the Tree Council to a national problem that turned out to be the consequence of mechanical hedge trimming. The lines of oak trees we see across a field are beautiful to look at and mark the line of a hedge in which they originally grew. It is job enough digging up the hedge, cutting down a series of mature oak trees is another order of magnitude. 'Mature' is the key word here. An oak sapling that puts its head above the hedge line now gets decapitated by the flail of the hedge trimmer. The Tree Council did a survey of hedge oaks and found a distribution in age that told us that they would eventually be consigned to history. Next time you go walking, picture the landscape without hedge oaks. Fortunately for us and for future generations, the Tree Council got onto the case and has set up the Real Hedge Fund to plant new hedges and hedge trees. It would be good if there could be a way of incentivising farmers to protect naturally occurring hedge oak saplings – but we can be sure it will not be quite on the scale of the bonuses paid to managers of banking hedge funds.

When asked, Donato has said that hawthorn makes the best hedging. It certainly has the thorns to help make it stock-proof, but it also has the

year's hazel owth

right sort of distribution of heartwood and sap wood, the right flexibility and the right vigour for good hedge laying. There are, however, many other hedge trees. Field maple is a common one and its butter-yellow leaves in October make our lanes a joy. Holly makes a dense evergreen hedge, bright with red berries in

September. Hazel is quick growing and provides such long shoots within a year's growth that they can be cut and used to make hurdle fences, trellises, baskets and barriers.

What has been found is that hedges of mixed species support more birds than hedges of single species, and that pure hawthorn hedges are better than pure elm or beech hedges. It was found in investigations which Max Hooper took part in 50 years ago that, if we reduce 15 miles of hedge to about 7 miles, the hedge will support the same numbers of birds but, if we reduce it by a further 3 miles, then there is just not enough nesting space and the number of birds is reduced.

Having reduced the miles of hedging by a peak rate in the 1960s of 10,000 miles per annum – an almost inconceivable rate – it became critical to know where and why there are mixed and pure hedges. Is it a case of soil type, farmer's preferences, management or trimming equipment? Answering these questions led Max Hooper to his finding, based on the observation of 227 dated hedges, that 70% of variation is explained by age: Saxon hedges tend to have 10-12 species of shrub and tree in them, enclosure hedges 1 or 2 species. Perhaps traditionally a hedge of one species of tree would be planted, but over the years more and more species crept in. Hooper's Hypothesis is that there is one species per 100 years. This makes walking in the countryside enormously more fun. It is impossible for me walking along a hedge not to count the different species within each 30-pace stretch. Boring, boring, boring to note that now the norm is to plant mixed-species hedges and that many more studies of hedges have been done and Hooper's Hypothesis is not a reliable predictor. We do not need to knock his science – he only said 70% of the variation is due to age – just build on and enjoy his insight, and keep in mind his findings on the importance of hedges in sustaining our wildlife.

Hedgelink is a 'partnership that brings everyone interested in hedgerows together, to share knowledge and ideas, to encourage and inspire, and to work with farmers and other land managers to conserve and enhance our hedgerow heritage'.

By being well informed we can help our decision makers to make the right choices.

Villages, woodlands and the countryside revisited

Wheathampstead revisited
(1) In Autumn 2010, I put together some photographs of Wheathampstead trees for the Wheathampstead Thursday Club. There was attractive autumn colour on the trees in the High Street - what a difference it made at what happened to be a time of unusually congested traffic!

Giant redwood

Goodness knows how I managed to miss the giant redwood on Mill Walk. The tree is within a few yards of the High Street, opposite The Bull. The rich red bark and upward curling foliage have the added charm of being on the river bank.

Pine at the platform

Also, when I was checking some facts about Mackerye End, I was put in touch with Patrick McNeill who chided me for not having included the 'magnificent pine on the station platform'. He said that it is visible from all round the valley. How did I come to miss that, too?

cnic area at
e station
atform,
iotograph
ken by Patrick
cNeill

I dutifully went to meet Patrick and clock the pine. I got more than I bargained for: Patrick introduced me to another six new tree nuggets.

The restored Wheathampstead station platform itself is a nugget, with a picnic area that is popular with local people in the summer as a place to eat a packed lunch and with children who race each other round and up and down the steps. I liked the story of a lad who comes with his grandfather, runs up the steps and across the platform calling 'Hello, George', pats the knee of the life-size carving of George Bernard Shaw and departs. The pine, we think, is a Corsican pine. Its bark is made up of smooth silver-and-pink strips on dark grey, towering up to dark green tufted foliage. Judging by its great girth and position on an embankment that was built to accommodate the platform in 1860, we reckon that it is about 150 years old.

Pine on Wheathampstead station platform

Many-specied sidings

Opposite the station, on the corner of Station Road and Lower Luton Road, were the railway sidings. There are 21 different species of tree in that one small space, now cared for by a volunteer ranger. That is a second new nugget.

Beautiful beech

The copper beech that stands in front of Wheathampstead Place by the bridge over the Lea is the third new nugget.

Historic boundary markers

The fourth new nugget is a line of mature oaks and field maples that are thought to have once marked the boundary of the Lamer estate. They line the bridleway on the north side of The Meads, the open space on either side of the River Lea.

Impressive oaks a field maples marʰ the boundary of Lamer estate

Indomitable willows

New squirrel-resistant sallow and coppiced sallow

The fourth new nugget is a plantation of goat willow (sallow) between the bridleway and the river. It was planted some fifteen years ago but became damaged by overcrowding, disease, and predatory squirrels. About half of the goat willows were removed two years ago and the rest were pollarded. In the space released, willows donated by Rothamsted Research were planted. These new willows are hybrids that are more resistant to disease and squirrels and, so far, have done well. In March 2018, the willows were pollarded again and the resulting willow poles were used to make spilings along the river bank – the sixth nugget.

Spilings

Sprouting spilings and uncut grass encourage people to use the access points

Spilings are a means of stemming river-bank erosion. Patrick's team of volunteers drove chestnut stakes into the river bed alongside the bank and then used the flexible poles from the pollarded willows to weave between the stakes to create what looks a bit like a fence – the 'spilings', 80 metres of them!

The spilings are sprouting with new growth. They do look attractive, and the sprouting willow and buffer zones of uncut grass along the bank encourage people – and dogs – to go in and out of the river at the access points only, thus reducing riverbank erosion.

Willow used as stakes as well as weavings

Willow can be used for the spiling stakes as well as for the weavings, as was done further along the River Lea in Batford. The willow stakes will take root and add strength. See how the earth is being banked right up to the spilings to encourage rooting.

Community orchard

Yes, there is yet another new nugget, the seventh. In 2012, Patrick spotted three ancient apple trees within a wilderness at the eastern end of The Meads and has managed with huge local support to create a community orchard there.

Old and new fruit trees in the orchard

In January 2014, 26 pear and apple trees, all native Hertfordshire varieties, were planted and by 2018 they are fruiting prolifically. The original three apple trees have been pruned and another local resident is the expert adviser on managing the orchard: winter pruning for shape and summer pruning to restrict growth. The orchard is located at the eastern end of The Meads, old and new apple trees and apple and pear fruiting in 2018.

Apple and pear trees fruiting in 2018

The Big Thing, to my mind, is the Wheathampstead community's involvement in the care and use of their trees. In each of the nugget projects local residents of all ages have been involved in enhancing amenities for all to enjoy: felling, pollarding and new planting in the willow plantation; installing the spiling; and creating the community orchard.

The Meads are only one of many public open spaces in Wheathampstead. I have given a flavour of the work done in one of them but cannot do justice to them all. To find out more about Bower Heath, Butterfield Nature Reserve,

Devils Dyke, Folly Fields, Nomansland, Marshalls Heath Nature Reserve, Gustard Wood, Melissa Field and The Dell, and how to get involved with the Wheathampstead Open Spaces Volunteers (WOSV), see http://www.wheathampstead-pc.gov.uk.

(2) I described the walnut tree next to the old school on Brewhouse Hill

in Wheathampstead as 'floppy'. The leaves are floppy, but the tree is not. It is a sturdy, large, lovely tree. Its bark is strikingly pale grey and attractively marked which complements the flint and brick markings on the adjacent old school building. Close by, there used to be a pub called The Walnut Tree; the bracket from which the pub sign used to hang is still there on the gable end of the

Walnut tree on Brewhouse Hill before the old school

house opposite the old school building and the turning into Bury Green. As at 2018, the pub-sign bracket is on the house that is the other half of Cunningtons lighting shop.

(3) See 'Fallen trees', below, to find out the fate of the Ash of Ash Grove.

(4) The red oak next to the children's play area in Canons Field succumbed to fungal disease and has been felled.

The red oak in Canons Field was magnificent, its leaves and their petioles characteristic of the species

(5) Botanists call the stalk between a leaf and twig a 'petiole'. In the context of oak trees, it is worth mentioning petioles because a distinguishing characteristic of the English oak, *Quercus robur*, is that the leaf sits on the twig: there is almost no petiole. On the other hand, its acorns are each on a stalk, giving rise to the tree being also referred to as the 'pedunculate oak': its acorn is on a foot (*ped*, Latin for foot).

Sandridge and Heartwood Forest revisited
(6) Where to start in conveying the wonderful progress and ongoing work being done at the Woodland Trust Heartwood Forest in Sandridge! It is impossible to do justice to it in this book, but I reiterate my encouragement to attend – and help at – the bluebell and Summer festivals; to visit Heartwood in all seasons; and to browse its website.

To give you a glimpse of some of the ongoing work at Heartwood, here is part of an address given by Brian Legg on Friday 25 May 2018:

'We have planted 600,000 of the 25 species of tree and shrub that are native to the UK and characteristic of Hertfordshire. The first to be planted, in the Winter of 2009–2010, are growing rapidly with some of the aspen, birch and willow now well over 6m tall. Many, especially the shrubs, are flowering and fruiting freely giving interest and colour to the forest throughout the Spring and Autumn.

'There are, however, about 60 species of tree and shrub native to the British Isles, and two years ago we planted a 26-acre arboretum with the full set. In total we planted 7,000 saplings and over 4,000 willow cuttings, so there are several hundred of most species. For centuries our trees and shrubs have been an essential source of food, animal feed, medicines, building materials, and high quality wood for sculptures and engraving, and the arboretum has been arranged to show these many uses. When you visit be sure to take a copy of the 48-page full colour guide with photographs and information about every native tree.'

Brian Legg
27 May 2018

Bricket Wood revisited
(7) I received a complaint! Fran Beak, who lives in Bricket Wood, said that, leafing through my book, she was delighted by the colourful photographs and looked forward to seeing her own Bricket Wood equally well represented. Her hopes were dashed: there were only two smallish photographs, both monotone, neither doing justice to arguably the most interesting and excitingly biodiverse area of the District.

It is impossible in this book to do full justice to Bricket Wood. I have chosen to focus on the ways in which trees, heathland, bogs and butterflies are interrelated. These are important aspects of Bricket Wood's contribution to biodiversity within the District – and the County.

Much of what was planned, and I reported on in 2010, has been implemented and is ongoing.

Judicious clearance lets in the light.

Boards have been laid so that people do not damage the valuable wetland habitats – and to give us access so that we can enjoy the Common.

Twelve longhorn cattle are loaned by a local farmer to graze heathland for six weeks in Spring and six weeks in Autumn. Their grazing keeps tree seedlings from turning the heath into woodland. Heathland is an important habitat for heathers and, in its boggy bits, for rare mosses.

Longhorns graze in the heathland enclosure twice a year (photograph by Chris Newman)

On and around the open heathland's moist, acid soil, alder buckthorn trees, *Frangula alnus*, thrive. The trees do not grow to much more than a couple of metres high. Their leaves are like those of dogwood but do not have much point at the tip nor veins that point inwards towards the tip. Most importantly, the leaves are food for Brimstone butterflies, yellow brimstones a flutter of sunshine in very early Spring.

Goat willow far left and alder buckthorn near right in the heathland enclosure

Also on the heathland, we see goat willow (pussy willow), *Salix caprea*, food of the Purple Emperor caterpillar.

Heathland is not the only area where goat willow thrives. There is a whole bank of them along the edge of the pond not far away.

Goat willow, food for Purple Emperor caterpillars, across the pond on Bricket Wood Common (photograph by Chris Newman)

Once the Purple Emperor butterflies emerge, they head for the highest tops of oak trees, and in Bricket Wood they find particularly tall oaks just the other side of the railway line in Mutchetts Wood. The male butterflies compete with each other for the best sunny spots, and to get to mate with the best females. Their 'competition' has been compared to the 'dog fights' of the Battle of Britain. It all takes place high above us so that it is a case of seeing not much more than what looks like some leaves fluttering about between the oak tops – but we know what is going on, and it is thrilling to be there. Bricket Wood butterfly conservationists will escort groups to experience this happening. Look out for such opportunities in July – and, in Spring, to have an exceptionally wide range of butterfly species pointed out and identified.

Gap in high oak canopy in Mutchetts Wood, Bricket Wood, where Purple Emperor butterflies are seen most frequently (photograph by Chris Newman)

The Purple Emperor females, having been won and mated with, need to head for the heathland and pond to find those goat willow leaves on which to lay their eggs.

I hope the residents of Bricket Wood will be pleased with the photographs I have chosen to show how colourful, as well as interesting and important, Bricket Wood is.

To find the pond, heathland, and the oaks where the male Purple Emperor butterflies gather, turn into School Lane from the main road through Bricket Wood, Mount Pleasant Lane, as it becomes Station Road close to the railway bridge. Continue along School Lane, passing several tracks off to the left. A mile from the start of School Lane is the well signed entrance to the Munden Estate. Immediately after that there is a layby where you can park a car. Retrace your steps and, opposite the entrance to the Munden Estate, is a wide all-weather path protected by low green bollards. This is the path you want. It is Public Bridleway 8

Turning on the left opposite Bridleway 8

Heading for the enclosure on Bridleway 8

from School Lane to Bucknalls Lane, part of the Hertfordshire Way. You can see the Bridleway on the map by the bollards. The pond with the Purple Emperors' goat willows is almost immediately on your right along a short path.

Heathland with alder buckthorn, more goat willow, heathers and mosses opens up to the left as soon as you pass the gate into the enclosure. If you are wondering what the concrete steps are at the gate, they are mounting blocks so that riders can dismount to open the gate and remount when they are through and have closed the gate.

To find the high oaks where the male Purple Emperors have their dog fights, continue along Bridleway 8, through the gate at the far side of the enclosure, until you go up and over a brick-sided railway bridge. Before the conifer hedge on the right, go down a path to your left immediately after the bridge. After about 20 yards there is a dead tree that has fallen on to another. If you stand next to it and look up on a warm day in mid July, you might just possibly see male Purple Emperor butterflies fluttering above you. For further needs of Purple Emperor butterflies, see 'Location location' in 'Tree management'.

(8) HSBC no longer have a training college at Hanstead House. The Park was sold in April 2012 to St Congar Land, a property development company 'with a general focus towards residential uses'. Plans were subsequently submitted to St Albans District Council for new dwellings and the conversion of Hanstead House. We await developments. Friends of Hanstead Wood continue to maintain the Wood and welcome visitors.

London Colney revisited
(9) The scientific name for our lovely native bird cherry tree is *Prunus padus.*

Redbourn revisited
(10) I have been told about a tree that is long gone but used to be a gathering place for Redbourn young people. 'See you at the 'Oly Boly', people would say. It was an ancient hollow oak on North Common. People would climb inside and up into its branches to watch the cricket and generally have a happy time together. The story gives us a glimpse of socialising in days before on-screen diversions.

(11) In his *Rural Rides*, William Cobbett writes of the trees between Redbourn and Hempstead as being 'very fine; oak, ashes and beeches; some of the finest of each sort'. He was riding on 24 June 1827 and also comments on the attractive flowers growing in the hedges. (Crook, 1970) See also a Cobbett connection to Roma Mills' robinia in 'Paul Arnolds trees planted for their historical connections'.

I often drive along the road between Redbourn and Hemel and imagine William Cobbett on his horse enjoying the fine trees and lovely hedges.

It is along this road, on the outskirts of Hemel but within the St Albans District, that an extensive housing and employment development is planned.

From the Local Plan 2018, we learn that St Albans and District is 81% Green Belt that cannot be built on except in defined circumstances. This area is designated Green Belt. There is tension between retention of Green Belt and the need for housing and associated employment and amenities.

Developers will be obliged by contract to retain important trees, provide strategic and local open space including managed woodland and ecological network links, a substantial new Country Park and a permanent green buffer to Redbourn.

The site borders on the M1 motorway. Trees could help to screen residents and workers from motorway noise and pollution.

The countryside revisited

(12) 'Set-aside' was introduced by the EU in 1988. It was intended to help reduce surpluses, and to deliver some environmental benefits – which it did. In 2008, following poor harvests that led to cereal shortages, the Scheme was abolished. Who knows what Brexit will bring.

(13) OPAL, the Open Air Laboratories Network, citizen science initiative, continues to thrive. Representatives continue to work with Heartwood.

OPAL funds the iSpot website that makes it easy to share and identify wildlife photographs.

Search on line for 'OPAL explore nature' to find out more.

(14) Donato has written his own explanation of how a hedge is laid: 'A cut is made at an angle at the base of a vertical trunk. The stem is carefully bent over to near horizontal. This becomes the 'pleacher'.

'Pleachers are held in position by vertical stakes and these are locked in position by twisted binders along the top.

'Stakes and binders are temporary, only serving to hold the pleachers in position until the new, living growth replaces them.'

(15) I love it that the hedge layers' rule of thumb as to when it is time for a hedge to be re-laid, is when the stems are the thickness of a boy's wrist.

(16) Donato Cinicolo, as at August 2018, has been Hertfordshire Hedge Laying Champion ten times.

(17) Heartwood are doing loads of hedge laying and teaching hedge laying. Do join in. They have chosen the Midlands method, not the Hertfordshire method of hedge laying.

Street trees and garden trees

When I started to look properly at the trees along our streets, I became aware of the contrast between the stretches where there are trees and those where there are only buildings, street signs and pavements(1).

As we come into St Albans on London Road, for example, there are banks of trees on either side: rounded ash trees, old hawthorns, full red horsechestnuts, pointed conifers, sturdy oaks. We pass under our fine ornamented iron railway

Weeping willow
and apple tree
at the bottom of
Holywell Hill are
lovely in spring

bridge and then it gets dreary where we have had something of a planning blight and there are no trees. Still on London Road and closer in to town, we did have a magnificent plane tree on the right at Marlborough Road but it is now shockingly damaged, its branches lopped to a dizzy height. However, further on, at an entrance to a car park on the left is a lovely pair of robinias, and on the right a clump of mixed conifers and broadleafs and then a line of pretty silver birches, the curve of their branches picking up the curve of the arched windows of the yellow and red brick building behind them. Here again, the townscape is being attractively softened and enhanced by trees.

From the Hemel Hempstead direction, we come into the City down Bluehouse Hill. Did you know that the avenue of good healthy maturing plane and maple trees on either side of the road and round the Redbourn roundabout is made up of 80 trees planted in 1980 to celebrate the Queen Mother's 80th birthday? Set into the flint wall at the turning from Bluehouse Hill into St Michaels, there is a plaque that tells us all about it.

The avenue of trees down Bluehouse Hill was planted to commemorate the Queen Mother's 80th birthday

Coming in from Redbourn we would have passed well kept hedges and the occasional hedge oak or line of oaks across a field. Then, on the Gorhambury side, we pass the grey cricket-bat willows, a beautiful line of tall limes, then poplars set further back, all preparing us for our first breathtaking view of St Albans Abbey ahead.

As we reach suburbia coming into St Albans on the Harpenden Road, there are some well established landscaped broadleafs in an open space behind a hedge on the right, then attractive enough pavement and garden trees on both sides of the road, followed by the exceptionally tall trees of Beech Bottom. The larches there, and on the diagonally opposite corner of the Ancient Briton intersection, are particularly distinctive. As we ascend the hill we are under an arch formed by dense woodland(2) on both sides of the road. Most of the trees have grown up since the 1930s and it is interesting to see how mature they are now. Out we come into the light where there is more open space and we can enjoy the trees as individuals.

At the top of the hill we join the road coming in from Sandridge which has passed up the long avenue of cherry trees, spectacular with alternating red and white blossom in the spring, and providing joyously upward-lilting branches through all seasons.

And so we are into St Peters Street and, on the right-hand side before and after our much admired horsechestnut at Chime Square, we have two strikingly shaped mature robinias. At all times of the year we can appreciate the quixotic zigzag of their branches. Opposite them on the left is a lovely

One of the two mature robinias on St Peters Street, this one by Chime Square

copper beech, and opposite that, on the corner of Grange Street, is a magnificent cedar of Lebanon above the low roof of the Pemberton Alms Houses.

Have you noticed, on the high blue-bricked pavement in front of the Hall Place wall on the left, the gnarled stubby sweet chestnut? It has been so trimmed that it is hardly more than an embraceable old trunk. Behind it – and behind the wall – are some spike-topped conifers, and beyond it we have St Peters churchyard's ash trees, limes and hazels.

A sweet chestnut outside Hall Place in St Peters Street

And then there are the young cherry trees of the memorial gardens.

You have to say something about the cherry trees at the top of the town. They are centred on the war memorial, you know. They are so beautiful and everyone sees them when they come to St Albans for the market or for something else.

Jim Cozens (born 1926)

Ornamental cherries by the war memorial in spring

THE REMARKABLE TREES OF ST ALBANS REVISITED

The cherry trees in the memorial gardens between the war memorial and St Peters church are magnificent with warm pink blossom in late April and with tawny crimson leaves in October. We were upset when the older cherry trees were removed but now, after only a few years, the new ones are stunning.

How bright and glossy green the plane trees are in the shopping part of St Peters Street, each tree a gift with its own dedication, all thanks to the Tree Sponsorship Scheme (see 'Trees and the future').

Right in amongst our city centre shops and banks and offices and churches there are trees to soften and lighten the scene.

Going out of the town down Catherine Street, the Scots pine against the skyline is iconic.

Going down Verulam Road we have the Gombards Alley copper beech dramatically set off by the adjacent yews (see 'Trees with history'); then pollarded limes followed by the spectacular cedar of Lebanon set against the Italianate church; Victoria Playing Field's lustrous-leaved planes, its vivacious limes, its variegated maple with soft green-and-white leaves and, finally, on the left, going upwards and away, is a whole bank of maroon, dark green and golden foliage.

Going out along Hatfield Road(3) we have neatly pollarded trees outside the University Faculty of Law, two tall sycamores outside the museum, the cedars and limes along the walls of Loreto College and, over the railway bridge, the huge horsechestnut, hollies and maples of Clarence Park.

Right: A light green holly tree makes a pleasing contrast to the bright pink brick of the Baptist Church in Upper Dagnall Street

Far right: A trimmed lime tree in Bricket Road draws our attention to the architecture of the building behind it

There is not much along Victoria Street. For more about that, see the MacMath's list in the introduction to 'Our favourite trees', and 'Trees and the future'.

Wherever we go in the suburbs of our District there are numerous attractive street trees:

> Jersey Farm was built in 1979 and the developer or the Council planted a lot of trees at that time. I think that without the trees, the brick and streets would have something hard about them. The trees soften the landscape and I constantly send a silent thank you to whoever planted them.
>
> Gill Curtis

That about sums it up, not only for Jersey Farm, but for all our areas of housing: there is not one housing area that is not tree-lined.

Ordinary trees in ordinary places, like this whitebeam in front of flats in London Colney, soften the street scene, filter the air cool our rooms in summer, let in the light in winter and give us something good to look at

Our major highways are lined with wonderful trees: the A414 North Orbital to the south of St Albans has great banks of trees on either side, as does the A1081 that takes us to the M25.

The Redbourn bypass has exceptionally attractive native trees including smaller varieties such as dogwood, which has white flowers in spring, white berries in autumn and eye-catching deep-red stems right through the winter months; spindleberry whose leaves are bright pink and fruits shocking pink and orange in autumn. There are also great sweeps of ash (much of it self-seeded, I suspect), and cherry and field maple and hawthorn – and some conifers, too. Rothamsted Research advised on the planting of the Redbourn bypass. They did a good job.

Not only does our District have street trees and highway trees, but we also have garden trees. Many of them are tucked out of sight but it is nice to know that they are there being enjoyed by their owners and neighbours. I know of a rare Chinese elm and an old yew out of general view.

Chinese elm
tucked away in an
inner city garden

In half-view are large old oak trees. We saw such a tree, Donato Cinicolo and I, when we were looking for the giant redwoods we had been told were in Cuckmans Drive in Chiswell Green. As we turned off the main road, we were gazing round and up and there was this amazing oaken canopy spreading above the houses behind a fence.

Even if we cannot see them, all these trees contribute to our well-being by absorbing carbon dioxide from the atmosphere and releasing oxygen into it.

The trees closer to the roads protect us by filtering car exhaust particulates, which are microscopic but solid particles of soot, carbon and fuel additives. When residents go in to do clearing jobs in the shelter belt of trees between London Road and their houses, they describe how filthy they get. Particulates are trapped by twigs and leaves and then washed to the ground by rain.

Also, some polluting gases are absorbed through the pores in the leaf surface. From research papers we learn:

... trees in Philadelphia, USA, have removed over 1,000 tons of air pollutants from the atmosphere in the year of 1994.

[It was] found that doubling the number of tree in the West Midlands would reduce excess deaths due to particles in the air by up to 140 per year.

Powe and Willis (2002)

Each tree has a huge surface area of leaves to do the job of air filtering which makes them an efficient resource – as well as being beautiful. And their beauty is not to be undervalued. It can be stressful driving along a busy road, being stuck in traffic, parking the car, lugging our shopping, labouring on a roadside, working in an office or at a desk at home, looking after children and other dependents – you name it, our occupations can intermittently become stressful.

Trees can lift our spirits even in winter and even in a large car park like this one at the London Colney hypermarket

It comes as no surprise to learn that measures of the physiological effects of stress have been found to be reduced more by views of nature than by views of urban scenes. In St Albans, you would be unlucky not to have a tree outside your office or house, and there would certainly be trees within a short walk.

All we have to do is look at them.

Opposite:
A tree to be seen from a window in New House Park

Street trees and garden trees revisited

(1) I described the various routes into St Albans by car and how the trees made our journey more pleasant and interesting.

As I was revisiting Verulamium Park and walking down the hill with the visible remains of the Roman wall on my left and the deep wide ditch on my right, I was impressed and thought that this entrance to St Albans deserved its own recognition.

The trees on either side do not give a cosy, welcoming feeling as does the avenue of maples leading into Batchwood, nor the uplifting feeling of the fan-vaulting-like trees of Lady Spencers Grove, rather they give an impression of towering strength and power. Fanciful, of course, but it is the sheer height and perpendicular quality of the trees that produce the effect.

The walk down the hill is an imposing overture to the charm of the lake with its swans and coots, attractive parkland, the quaint Fighting Cocks, and the open view of the Abbey as we climb the hill to the City.

(2) To get your bearings, the 'dense woodland' on either side of Harpenden Road between the traffic lights at the Ancient Briton and the intersection with Heath Farm Lane on the left and Edmund Beaufort Drive on the right coming up the hill, is part of Bernards Heath.

(3) Going out along Hatfield Road there have been some changes in use of buildings close to the city centre: the 'University Faculty of Law' is now a primary school and the 'museum' is now a housing development. Some of the trees along the street line have had to go.

Tree management

Coppicing, pollarding and pruning

Coppicing and pollarding have been carried out by humans ever since they wanted to use wood for construction, for tools and for firewood and found that certain trees would re-grow after being cut.

Five thousand years ago, our ancestors would manage the woodland(1) they lived in by tackling about an acre at a time each year, leaving standard oaks to grow tall but coppicing other trees. At any given time there would be habitats for insects, grubs, animals and plants that like the light (in newly coppiced areas), for those that like half light (areas coppiced some years before), and for those that like the semi-gloom of a full canopy (areas due to be coppiced soon).

Opposite:
Management of roadside trees for our pleasure and safety is a mammoth and expensive task

A standard oak and coppiced hornbeam

It was biodiversity heaven.

In Hertfordshire, right up until the last century, ancient hornbeam and oak woodland such as Langley Wood (now within Heartwood Forest), Batchwood, part of Bricket Wood, Symondshyde, and many others round our District, were managed in this way. The hornbeam wood was typically made into charcoal and sold to London for firewood: hornbeam was called 'Hertfordshire gold'(2) for the money it made the county and it is said that 'London bread was baked on Hertfordshire hornbeam'.

Two years' growth after coppicing

In ancient woodland like Batchwood and Langley Wood, we see the regular banks that formed where our ancestors used the brash from the trees they had coppiced to build up barriers to protect the coming new growth from browsing animals. The barriers surrounded the newly coppiced area, and the same lines would be used about 20 years or so later, as again that patch was coppiced, and again the brash barrier formed: again and again for millennia, with the brash debris gradually building up into the banks we see today.

Coppicers would also use the brash to make 'wigwams' round the coppiced stools (stumps) to doubly protect the new shoots from being eaten by animals. We still do that today. In woodland in Ayot St Lawrence, the Woodland Trust St Albans Support Group built, to good effect, wigwam-style protectors around the newly coppiced stools. And we saw the proper hazel baskets round coppiced stools that the Friends of Batchwood created.

Pollarding differs from coppicing in that the cutting is done high enough for the new growth to be clear of grazing animals, either wild ones like deer or domesticated ones like sheep or cattle, so saving all that protection work of wigwams or baskets and brash barriers.

Pollarding needs to be done in the right season, in a way sympathetic to the needs of the tree, its natural

An ancient pollard hornbeam

growth tendencies, its species, and the way it has been pollarded previously. In fact, once a tree has been pollarded, it needs to be pollarded again at the right time intervals. After regular pollarding the pollard heads become too weak to support a crown and the tree's life would be shortened if pollarding did not continue regularly.

Pollarding was not always done for the sole purpose of using the branch wood. For example, a tree might be pollarded to stand out as a boundary marker. This is unwise as, even after a single cutting, the multiple stems that grow after pollarding, if left to grow indefinitely, can become huge but not

A wonderful
pollarded
sycamore

carry the foliage needed to sustain the tree as a whole, and the tree's life is shortened rather than lengthened. This is the case for an extraordinary sycamore within a private development in St Albans. It is a wonderfully venerable and substantial tree, but one-off pollarding, perhaps to mark a boundary, has reduced its capacity to support the crown it needs to sustain it comfortably.

Pollarding nowadays is spoken of by the Royal Horicultural Society as 'a method of pruning, useful if you need to limit the size of a tree that it is too near a house, has too wide a shade, or is on a street and would get in the way of streetlights, telegraph posts and wires'. This is not specifically 'pollarding'. In pruning that is not pollarding, the new growth continues through existing shoots. While we were photographing in Clarence Park, Donato Cinicolo showed me a copper beech in York Road that had recently been pruned well.

He pointed out that new growth was coming from shoots that had been left at the end of slender branches. It is difficult for a tree surgeon to reach those slender ends of the branches and it would be easier to cut the branch lower, but a good tree surgeon knows that, for mature trees like this one, it is best not to cut back below existing shoots that can carry on new growth.

A perfect pruning cut

The new growth after coppicing or pollarding is juvenile growth from under the bark rather than from within the tree. The managers of the trees in Hatfield Park claim(3) that some of their oaks are more than 900 years old and put their longevity down to their pollarding.

One more thing: after standard oaks were felled, a single shoot of new growth from the stool would be selected and all other shoots cut back. The next standard would therefore come from the bole and root system of the original tree rather from a seeded sapling.

So we need not panic as some of us do when trees are being cut back. When Paul Arnold was working for the City Parks Department he was responsible for pollarding in Salisbury Avenue, St Albans. When he came back to the work after a lunch break he found a huge notice on the fence 'Council vandals'. He had meetings with the residents and explained that it was analogous to a hair cut or trimming our nails, but we cannot help but think of it as having

Pollarded trees in
Salisbury Avenue,
Harpenden

St Peters fig tree
after pruning

our own limbs cut off. We shall not know what the tree feels but we can console ourselves with the thought that good pollarding or pruning is prolonging its life.

Trees in Salisbury Avenue, Harpenden, and New House Park, St Albans, are pollarded. Harpenden residents regularly express their concern to the Trees and Woodlands section of the Council. Not every tree is cut back every year: cutting takes place every year but alternate trees are left until the following year. This is the theory but it does look to me as if it is not quite alternate trees. Presumably the selection of which trees' turn it is each year is a bit more complex than 'alternate'.

Sometimes it is a case of being patient and waiting for abundant fresh growth as in the case of the trees that were cut down along the railway embankments and at the end of Everlasting Lane – and the fig tree in St Peters churchyard which I panicked about when I saw how little of it there was left after pruning. It was thriving a season later.

If it's got to go, it's got to go

Rotten centre
of the old oak
that grew in The
Quadrant car
park

Trees occasionally have to be removed completely because they are diseased or dying and have become dangerous. Where possible, they are left to die naturally and the stumps provide food for beetles, homes for animals and sounding boards for woodpeckers.

Sometimes it is a case of mourning a sad but inevitable loss. This is all we could do when our wonderful oak tree in the Marshalswick Quadrant car park was cut down. It was rotten in its core and could have caused serious injury or damage if even part of it had collapsed. Imagine the letters to the paper if a person's car had been crushed, let alone a person killed.

I did wonder in the case of the Marshalswick Quadrant oak whether it would not have been possible to test if particular branches were at risk and remove them rather than the whole tree and, at the Rothamsted Research open day in May 2010, we could see the results of thermal imaging that had been done on the magnificent copper beech in the manor gardens. This did show where there is healthy growth and where there are areas of concern. Presumably the imaging is expensive and the Quadrant property owners may not have felt the expenditure justifiable. If they knew how upset people would be at the loss of the tree they might have reconsidered. When I was calling for the community to share their favourite tree, again and again people would tell me how upset they were that the beautiful oak in the Quadrant had been cut down.

Sometimes we do not want a tree. It might be too near our house, its roots might be causing bricks in the pavement to rise so that people trip and fall, we might feel we cannot cope with clearing away its leaves in autumn, or find that the sticky stuff from the aphids it attracts is ruining our car or our carport roof. Usually there is a way round these challenges.

More tricky are the issues around development. A tree preservation order can mean that property cannot be developed profitably. In St Albans, the area along Victoria Street that includes the police station, the Friends burial grounds, the tall building below the magistrate's court and the car park on the corner of Bricket Road is available for development and is a case in point. We have to decide what we want for such a central site. Are we willing to lose the beautiful copper beech on the corner, the lovely fountaining silver birch, the two magnificent plane trees and the liquidambar within the site? (See 'Plane perfect' in 'Our Favourite trees'.) Or do we badly need hotel accommodation and more car parking in the city centre? The decisions are complicated.

I have been fascinated to learn that what sounded like a good idea, a sports centre with rifle range, was turned down by local residents in favour of the natural open space of the Jersey Farm Woodland Park. The seemingly reasonable idea of Aboyne

Copper beech within a development area

Lodge School moving into the not very exciting space between Folly Lane and Verulam Road was rejected by local residents in favour of keeping Victoria Playing Field as a park. Making the wall on Verulam Road safe at least cost was campaigned against by residents until a solution was found that would save the ancient yew trees behind it. These examples show how much St Albans people value trees and nature and are prepared to fight for them. We should be proud of ourselves.

On a light note, someone phoned the Council and irately objected to the tree recently planted on the verge by their garden. The problem? The petals from the blossom in spring. One man's joy can be another man's bane.

Traditional orchards

(This section was contributed by David Curry.)(4)

Traditional orchards, a much loved part of our British heritage and countryside, support a wide range of wildlife due to the mosaic of habitats they encompass including fruit trees, standing and fallen dead wood, scrub and hedgerows. Surveys have shown that orchards provide a refuge for over 1800 species spanning the plant, fungi and animal kingdoms. The noble chafer, *Gnorimus nobilis*, one of our rarest beetles is associated with old orchards where it is dependent on old decaying wood within live trees especially apple, plum and cherry.

Often occupying the same piece of land for centuries and managed without any chemical input, these sites were hotspots for biodiversity, but they are now under serious threat. It is for this reason that the UK Biodiversity Action Plan (BAP) now includes traditional orchards.

Historical data show that the orchard area across England has declined by over 56% since 1950. In Hertfordshire initial indicators show a decline of 58% in the number of orchard sites in the county over the past 100 years with most of the surviving orchards being in relatively poor condition. Many of these orchards would have contained fruit varieties local to Hertfordshire with the result that many local varieties of fruit may have been lost.

The Hertfordshire Orchard Initiative was established in 1998 in response to the rapid decline of Hertfordshire's orchards and fruit heritage. It is run by a group of Local Government Officers, orchard owners and wildlife experts to enable and support the conservation and management of Hertfordshire's fruit orchards and cultivars and promote healthy eating. More information can be found at www.hertfordshireorchardinitiative.org.uk.

What we can learn from oak trees

The issues are wider than saving attractive trees or even open spaces in city centres. A few thoughts on oak trees illustrate the inter-dependency of species, and the care we need to take to preserve ecological balance and biodiversity.

Under the strictest definition of native – those trees which flourished before Britain was cut off from the rest of Europe about 10–12,000 years ago – there are only 33 trees agreed by all to be within that definition and the English oak, *Quercus robur*, is one of them. It is a tall strong slow-growing long-lived tree that characterises our countryside.

The bark provides a purchase for mosses and lichens and there are some 500 species of invertebrates that depend on oak trees in one way or another (Miles, 2006 and Lipscombe & Stokes, 2008). That is 500 different species, not 500 invertebrates. There are tens of thousands of invertebrates in the average oak, and birds and bats, shrews and hedgehogs come to feed on them. They build their nests in the oak, hide in the hollows round their roots and hibernate under their leaves. The Purple Hairstreak butterfly breeds solely on oak trees: no oaks, no Purple Hairstreaks (Dunk, 1985).

Gall wasps

Gall wasps have a particularly interesting relationship with oaks. It is they that are responsible for the ever-present oak apples, scaled artichoke galls and the smooth marble galls on leaf buds, the tiny round spangle galls under the leaves, knopper galls in acorns and the currant galls on flowers of oak trees. The astonishing thing is that the galls are the oak's defence against the penetration of the wasp into its tissue to lay her eggs but, in defending itself by manufacturing mutated tissue round the eggs, the oak provides the larvae that will hatch from the eggs with the nutrients and

Oak galls

protection that they will need. And for each species of gall wasp, the oak provides the species-specific requirements for those grubs. (Miles 2006)

So far it seems that, in the case of most of the gall wasps, the oak has to expend a bit more energy in wrapping a protective coating round their eggs but they are no real threat to the tree. However, knopper gall wasps are a problem because they go for acorns and, if knopper gall wasps got the upper hand, the ability of oaks to reproduce might be compromised. How did it come about that the knopper gall wasp evolved to be a threat? You knew it would be our fault: we introduced Turkey oaks and the knopper gall wasp life cycle depends on the Turkey oak and the English oaks in alternate years.

The first lesson, therefore, is a double one: native trees are a Good Thing because they have co-evolved with our other species, able to benefit them but also to protect themselves from their harmful effects; and we need to be vigilant when we introduce new species of tree, just as we know to be vigilant in introducing new insect species.

Location location

A second lesson is: we have to be careful how we muck about with where trees are.

An illustration of this is a study of the Purple Emperor butterfly. Like the Purple Hairstreak, the Emperor lives in oak trees. It is to be found in the topmost branches. The male Purple Emperor butterfly comes down from the top canopy to drink the mineral-rich juices of dung or carrion and the female, after mating, lays her eggs on goat willow leaves, *Salix caprea*, also known as 'sallow'. Goat willow is a shrubby tree found in woods and heaths and marshland or by ponds. The implication is that it is all very well planting our beautiful oaks in towns but we need to keep the ones near pasture, near woodland and near water, where Purple Emperor butterflies can find the other material they need to carry on the generations.

We can now add a third lesson: wildlife has complicated multi-dependencies, many of which we cannot yet know let alone understand, so that we had better be careful what we get rid of.

Good guys, bad guys

Advantage is not all on the side of the creatures that live off the oaks. Birds and small mammals, particularly, are useful to oaks. Jays carry acorns far and wide and hide them in just the right way for later germination. 'It has been observed' (just imagine the project) that a single jay can squirrel away 5,000 acorns in a ten-week period (Miles, 2006).

Who mentioned squirrels!

Now, grey squirrels really are a menace to oak trees. We saw in Batchwood the damage they can do. Does it add insult to the injury to know that tearing the bark in this way is a form of male squirrel display?

Lammas growth

Oaks have a specific ability to produce a second set of foliage in midsummer. It is bright green or reddish, which contrasts strongly with the existing matured dark green foliage. It happens around the beginning of August and, 1 August being Lammas Day in the church calendar, the new growth is known as Lammas growth.

One theory is that the Lammas growth is a consequence of moth-larvae infestations that cause a loss of leaves – which shows that, given time, trees can evolve and deal with threats. It also illustrates the co-evolution of tree and insects.

Lammas growth

Another perspective is that Lammas growth may by a case of adding more manufacturing capacity when energy allows in late summer. In general, in temperate regions with seasons like ours, trees get all their leaves out and up manufacturing nutrients as early as possible after the risk of frost. That is the way to take maximum advantage of the sunshine required for photosynthesis before sap must be withdrawn so that it does not freeze in the cold winter.

Whatever the trigger for the Lammas growth, it is a manifestation of adaptation to native conditions by a native tree, confirming our need to foster our precious native species: they are the ones that can hang on in there when the going is tough.

Altogether

Altogether, considering the inter-dependency of species and the effect of factors we might not dream of, we need to think twice before interfering with an environment that has reached a balance over a very long time.

Horsechestnut leaf-miner damage

Leaf-miner moth grubs are attacking our horsechestnuts

Moving on from oak trees, no one can have failed to notice that the leaves of our horsechestnuts are turning brown long before autumn. This is because leaf miner moths come out of the ground round the base of the tree, climb up the trunk and lay their eggs on the leaves. The eggs hatch and the grub mines its way through the leaf munching on its nutrients and depriving the tree of proteins. It is said not to be life-threatening but it does weaken the tree.

You may have seen BBC footage in January 2010 of the efforts to protect the horsechestnut trees in the magnificent avenue across Boxmoor, Hemel Hempstead. Rather than attacking the moth, the experts helped the tree to survive the invasion by injecting(5) nutrients under pressure into the soil around the tree.

There is a suggestion that the red horsechestnut might be resistant to the leaf miner moth. The red horsechestnut (*Aesculus x carnea*) is a cross between the North American red buckeye (*Aesculus pavia*) and the common horsechestnut (*Aesculus hippocastanum*). The red horsechestnut is smaller overall and has smaller leaves, which are often a bit puckered or twisted – and it has pink flowers. They are quite a popular hybrid and you may know of one. You can play a part in research to defend our horsechestnuts by keeping an eye open for red horsechestnuts and reporting to St Albans District Council Tree Warden Scheme on the extent to which they are being invaded by leaf miner moth.

Tree management revisited

(1) I have long known and loved our local ancient oak and coppiced-hornbeam woodland: Langley Wood in Sandridge, Bricket Wood Common, Batchwood and more. They have shaped my conception that Neolithic humans lived here in such woodlands, coppicing hornbeam for fuel, using oak timber to build shelters, and feeding themselves by foraging for fruits and nuts.

This conception has been challenged in multiple ways.

Our local woodlands are designated 'ancient woodland' but the official definition of ancient woodland is woodland that has existed since 1600 AD.

Oliver Rackham tells us that it is difficult to survive only on the produce of a forest (Rackham, 2006).

Rowe and Williamson tell us that pollen evidence shows that hornbeam was poorly represented in Hertfordshire's prehistoric landscape (Rowe and Williamson, 2013).

It is from the 17th century onwards that there is good documentary evidence of Hertfordshire supplying London with the hornbeam faggots and charcoal that generate such high-temperature heat.

I began to wonder whether the 'ancient' woodlands that I know and love were perhaps cultivated to feed London's demand in relatively recent centuries, and bear absolutely no relation to woodland in Neolithic times.

What landscape did Neolithic people find when they arrived here after the ice had retreated?

I find that there are still differing models of the nature of 'wildwood' and what the landscape looked like across southern Britain in Neolithic times: dense trees from coast to coast, or a varying mix of tracts of dense trees interspersed with grassland (Rackham, 2006).

All agree that vegetation was affected by the grazing of wild deer, wild horses, wild cattle and wild pigs and that these animals were domesticated by Neolithic man.

In St Albans and District, we need to think of the effect of varying topography and of varied soil textures, fertility and acidity (Rowe and Williamson, 2013).

Rosalind Niblett can tell us about our immediate landscape when the Romans arrived. She quotes grains of pollen preserved in the peat and silts of the flood plain of the Ver as evidence that along this valley any 'primeval forest cover had long since been replaced by pasture and cornland' (Niblett, 1995).

In the century before the Roman invasion, Iron Age people were growing crops and raising sheep, cattle and horses. They were also extracting iron from iron-rich clay, making tiles and pottery and weaving on looms (Ibid.). These activities would have needed the resources to be found in woodland: springy ash branches to turn pottery wheels, fuel for furnaces (perhaps hot-burning hornbeam) and spindle whorls for looms.

We therefore find that 2000 years ago, if not 5000 years ago, people here were living in a mix of arable, pasture and woodland: arable in the valleys, woodland on the higher ground and animals being herded up and down between the two levels for pasturing (Rowe and Williamson, 2013).

I find it remarkable that I can still see this pattern as I walk in our local countryside: fields bounded by hedges across the valleys and woodland on the hill tops.

And what of the period after the Romans?

Anglo Saxon records show that woods were valuable property and were used for keeping pigs and as a source of fuel but most countryside was being farmed (Rackham, 2006).

The Doomsday Book measures woodland in terms of how many pigs it could feed, not an easy measure to interpret. About half of the settlements recorded possessed woods (Ibid.).

We learn that 'great oak woods were preserved by the monks chiefly for the acorns they produced to feed the pigs' (Tomkins, 1967).

With the dissolution of the monasteries, however, new landowners 'taking less thought for the future and wanting not woods but park, felled so many of the old trees that laws had to be passed to stop their indiscriminate felling' (Ibid.).

Perhaps unexpectedly, industrialisation and urbanisation extended rather than reduced the amount of managed woodland. While woodland is valuable, it is maintained. Hence the many hornbeam-coppiced woods in the District.

Today we are aware of the value of woodlands and of keeping them connected by hedges so that wildlife – and we – can thrive. We know now that we depend on trees. David Curry says it all in his Foreword.

I recommend the Heartwood Forest Landscape History Walks. We are taken to a vantage point and encouraged to imagine the changes in the landscape from the time when plants came out of the oceans to the present day. Look out for them at https://heartwood.woodlandtrust.org.uk/.

(2) Roger Miles has challenged me to give the source for my statement that hornbeam was known as 'Hertfordshire gold' for the money it made for the County economy. I have to confess that I have not been able to find the term quoted in print.

Let me know if you find a source for the term – or tell Roger who likes it but, quite rightly, doesn't feel he can use it without a reference to quote.

(3) The oak trees in Hatfield Park being 900 years old has been confirmed by dendrochronology.

(4) David Curry has since moved to his hometown, Plymouth. He continues to protect urban forest – including orchards.

(5) When trees are not thriving, it is sometimes because the soil has become compacted. Tree root growth is inhibited if oxygen in the soil around its roots falls below 10–15%. Air and the mycorrhizal fungi that facilitate the uptake of nutrients by roots, can be injected under pressure to relieve compaction and help tree roots access nutrients.

Also, there are ways to prevent compaction and allow moisture to reach the soil around urban trees.

Trees and the future

The Tree Strategy and Policy for St Albans was written within in the context of the Council's vision

> to preserve and enhance the distinctive character of St Albans city and District, making it an outstanding place to live, work and enjoy.

Many things make St Albans and St Albans District an outstanding place to live, work and enjoy – and the trees are one of them. I find I am not the only member of the community who thinks so. At two meetings I attended in the week of writing this, I was struck by how big an issue trees are for us: at a St Albans Civic Society meeting on the 'Past present and future of the Abbey Theatre', substantial time was spent on the trees that will be lost when the adjacent swimming pool is built; and at a talk on 'English Heritage and Verulamium Park', the loss of trees and concern for their replacement was the topic most passionately discussed.

Policy 1 of the Trees and Woodlands five-year plan is to 'ensure that the tree population continues to be developed and expanded with new planting where appropriate'.

Policy 2 emphasises the value of planting native species to maximise habitats for wildlife.

Policy 3 is a commitment to promote community understanding and ownership of our trees.

You will know from what I have written throughout this book that I support all of the above policies and want us to help the Council to fulfill the aims that the policies imply.

In these times of austerity, it is going to be difficult for the Council to fulfill the aim stated in the Tree Strategy:

> Many of our most notable tree-lined streets have tree populations that are over-mature.

> ...new trees should be introduced between the mature trees to ensure that there will be continuous tree cover in future years.

...the massive contribution that large trees make to the character of the environment must be maintained and safeguarded and be supported by new planting of similar species [forest type species]

The council will place a priority on the replacement of ageing street tree populations...planting large growing trees where appropriate.

This all adds up to a burden on resources to acquire the trees, to plant them and to look after them.

How can we help?

As individuals

Lots of individuals and groups are planting new trees and looking after them:

(1)The Friends of Batchwood, the Friends of Victoria Playing Fields, the Friends of Hanstead Wood, the Friends of St Peters, and the Hertfordshire Orchard Initiative, for example, are doing sterling work. The Friends of Verulamium are desperate to unblock whatever it is that is holding up the planting of trees to replace the two hundred trees – yes, 200 – they state in their newsletter that the Park has lost.

Private individuals are doing their bit by planting trees in their gardens. Elaine and Roger Tate, for example, wanted a shelter belt between their home and the M1 motorway and, with the help of the Countryside Management Service, the Forestry Commission, the Woodland Trust St Albans Support Group, their friends and their own hard work, have managed to plant and will look after 850 trees.

We need to keep up the good work but also recognise that we can do something more.

This is where the Tree Sponsorship Scheme and the Tree Warden Scheme come in.

The Tree Sponsorship Scheme(2) – planting new trees

It all started when the magnificent lime tree avenue in St Peters Street became of such an age that it was decided that the trees had to go. The original avenue of limes made the town centre truly beautiful in summer.

St Peters Street, St Albans, a century ago: 'One of the loveliest boulevards in Europe'

THE REMARKABLE TREES OF ST ALBANS REVSITED

Elsie Toms tells us that St Peters Street was referred to as 'one of the loveliest boulevards in Europe', and that the St Peters Street lime trees were planted in 1881 at the expense of a private citizen, Mr H. Gotto (Toms, 1962).

But vwoop! They were all cut down and dug out.

It was Eric Roberts, then chairman of the Civic Society, who proposed a scheme of sponsorship to offset the huge expenditure required to replace all the trees. Eric had seen such a scheme work well in Folkestone.

The idea was that we could sponsor a tree by making a set financial contribution and the Council would commit to acquire the tree, plant it maintain it, and even replace the tree if required.

St Peters Street
now

The Scheme was amazingly successful with many individuals, groups, schools, businesses and organisations contributing to it. All but one of the trees in our wonderful avenue of plane trees in St Peters Street was given under the Tree Sponsorship Scheme. If it had not been for the Scheme, St Peters Street – and St Albans – would be a very different place.

It had been foreseen that people would want to dedicate the tree in some way. Rather than commemorative plaques, a Tree Book of Remembrance was created and, for each tree, there is a page of commemoration with a beautiful hand-painted illustration of the tree – or some leaves and fruit of the tree – together with the dedication message written in perfect calligraphy. The illustrations and calligraphy were done by Linda Williams.

Councillor Bill Morris was just one of the other people who worked to see the limes replaced. 'Trees are the living furniture of our streets' is the dedication he gave to the tree that he sponsored.

St. Albans and District
Tree Book of Remembrance

Sponsored by St. Albans Civic Society
as part of a partnership with
St. Albans City and District Council.

Calligraphy and Illustration by Linda Williams.
Book made by I. R. Dorset of 'By George' 1999.

The title page of
the Tree Book of
Remembrance

Some trees commemorate a new birth or a person's life, some an event, a personal or family celebration, an idea or a thought or a success. Many commemorated the new millennium.

The range of tree species planted is impressive: beech, copper beech, silver birch, larch, oak, sweet gum (liquidambar), snowy mespil (no, I don't know it either), wild cherry, field maple, hawthorn, Crimean lime, flowering crab [apple], golden hornet, white mulberry, walnut and London plane.

As well as the city centre, sponsored trees were planted in Ragged Hall Lane, Netherway, Alpin Close, Forefield, Ramsey Close, Woodland Drive, Hatfield Road, Hamilton Road, Marquis Lane, Rothamstead Park, Clarence Park and Verulamium Park.

The dedications are inspirational and we can read them for ourselves if we ask at reception in the Council offices to see the Tree Book of Remembrance. Here are some of the dedications:

No said the bird, for the leaves were full of children hidden excitedly containing laughter

With gratitude for 21 years as Cathedral Organist and 40 years in St Albans

Happy years living in St Albans

'A fool sees not the same tree that a wise man sees,' Wm Blake

In celebration of Friendship and Goodwill – deep roots and many branches

For the Pleasure of Future Generations

To maintain a green heart in our City

For tomorrow

A record of gratitude for our Civic Heritage

As a living symbol of the role of Soroptimist International as a global voice for women

For a green St Albans. To recall the success of the 'Save Gombards Yew Group' and the help of Diane Fear

Rainbows Brownies and Guides: Future citizens of St Albans

To capture the beauty of Autumn

For the privilege of being mayor. 'The leaves of the tree are for the healing of the nations' Revelations 22:2.

In 1999, a tree could be sponsored for £50, or more depending on the species of tree. This is much less than it costs the Council to acquire, plant and maintain the tree but it is at least a contribution towards the cost. The Tree Sponsorship Scheme gave us the avenue of planes in the main street of our city and many more trees along our streets and in our parks.

What of it now?

The St Albans Civic Society has a fund set aside to produce the pages of the Tree Book of Remembrance but it has not been called on for some years. At the time of writing, I have been told that there will be a meeting at the Council to discuss the Scheme.

A St Peters Street plane 'For a green St Albans. To recall the success of the Save Gombards Yew Group' and the help of Diane Fear'

For a green St. Albans

To recall the success of the 'Save the Gombards Yews Group' and the help given by Diane Fear.

London Plane
St. Peter's Street
2001

Victoria Street used to be an avenue too. Would its restoration be too ambitious an aim for the revival of the Tree Sponsorship Scheme?

How Victoria
Street used to be

The Tree Warden Scheme(3) – looking after trees

Tree wardens are a national force of local champions and a key part of the Tree Council's community action programme which gives people who feel that trees matter an opportunity to:

- champion their local trees and woods;
- plant and care for trees by watering new planting and replacing tree ties;
- carry out woodland management;
- set up tree nurseries using seed collected locally;
- survey local trees;
- provide early warning of threats, disease, decay and vandalism;
- involve their neighbours in tree projects;
- get together with like-minded people for training and field trips;
- spearhead Tree Council initiatives.

If you would like to join the St Albans Tree Warden Scheme, contact the Scheme co-ordinator at treewardens@stalbans.gov.uk.

Together we can ensure that we pass on to future generations trees as remarkable as those that we inherited.

Trees and the future revisited

(1) What was I thinking of not to include the Friends of Bernards Heath in the list of groups doing truly sterling work in planting new trees and managing existing ones.

Nor did I know to include the Wheathampstead Open Spaces Volunteers.

(2) The Tree Sponsorship Scheme is thriving. In early 2018, four of us clubbed together to sponsor a tree to commemorate our friendship. Our tree is in Clarence Park, a flowering cherry, *Prunus avium* 'Plena'. Its flower is double and white, and its first leaves in spring are bronze. We have a delightfully illustrated page in the Tree Book of Remembrance on display in the Council foyer and the Council will look after our tree and replace it if need be.

Go online to the St Albans and District website, search for 'sponsor a tree', read the terms and conditions, download the form and away you go.

(3) The St Albans District Council Tree Warden scheme invites the St Albans community to contribute to the on-line registration of St Albans trees and tagging of those trees that have 'community value'. If you would like to contribute by nominating a tree for tagging or by helping to register the trees, please email treewardens@stalbans.gov.uk and join in on training sessions.

Registration of the trees will be on 'Treezilla', a platform for citizen science that has been devised by the Open University. The idea is to map every tree in Britain and create a data-rich platform on which a wide range of citizen science investigations can be built. Anyone can register a tree, but it would be good to do it together as a community.

The Defra 25 Year Environment Plan 2018 lists 10 key objectives:

1 Clean air
2 Clean and plentiful water
3 Thriving plants and wildlife
4 Reducing the risks of harm from environmental hazards
5 Using resources from nature more sustainably and efficiently
6 Enhancing beauty, heritage and engagement with the natural environment
7 Mitigating and adapting to climate change
8 Minimising waste
9 Managing exposure to chemicals
10 Enhancing biosecurity

There is only one item on this list where I cannot think of a way in which trees can contribute to meeting the objective.

It cannot be stressed too strongly: trees are our future.

Fallen trees

As I gazed at Donato's photographs of fallen trees, again and again they struck me as fallen heroes, occasionally as bloody torsos, sometimes as battling on determinedly despite being wounded, sometimes as sacrificing themselves to the needs of the birds and invertebrates essential to the continuing cycle of life.

Verulam Golf Club oak

How dignified and imposing this oak relic manages to look.

It will be habitat to a host of different organisms for a very long time.

It is on the edge of a Verulam Golf Club fairway.

Beech at the west front of the Abbey

Our magnificent beech at the west front of the Abbey has lost a limb. The limb crushed a wall and landed on a footpath. The tree itself is looking good: its foliage a bright healthy green, its mast prolific, and its monstrous roots,

Left:
Relic of an oak tree on the Verulam Golf Club course

Beech tree at the west front of the Abbey in 2018

that look as if they belong to a dinosaur, are hosting little yew and holly seedlings.

People walk under its canopy constantly, so it is going to have to have a fitness test. We must savour its beauty while we can.

Cherry in Sandridge Road

'Truncated' is a term we use in several different contexts. It seems apt for the remains of this cherry tree. The tree's life has been truncated, the remains were the trunk of the cherry tree so that the tree was literally truncated, and it looks horrifyingly like a severed torso – or trunk - of a giant person.

Close-to we see the exquisite sheen of its bark, the glow of the resin it has extruded and the complexity of its vascular system as it has aged into wood, heartwood and a hollow.

Remains of a Sandridge Road cherry tree

Robinia in French Row

It's the worst thing! What can be worse than watching a living thing battling to survive, gradually collapsing from the inside and having to be cut down. Oh dear. That has been the fate of the Robinia at the end of French Row. And it was once so beautiful and seemingly healthy.

As at August 2018, we have a stump, and hopes of a replacement sapling that we can grow to love.

Decline and fall of the Robinia at French Row

Mackerye End chestnut

We can still see the characteristic spiralling of sweet chestnut bark in a desiccated old trunk in the grounds of Mackerye End House, Wheathampstead. Are the green leaves at its side from a separate seedling or are they sprouting from the old wood?

The splaying ends of the trunk are a work of art – and home to much wildlife.

Beautiful sweet chestnut log

Woodland Drive oak

It could neither be predicted nor prevented. No wonder the fall of a branch of the majestic oak in Woodland Drive was designated 'an act of God'.

From the branch base left on the tree, it looks as if the tree has lost a minor limb but the branch lying across the neighbours' gardens is immense.

A branch fell in February 2018 from an oak tree in Woodland Drive

Horsechestnut in Verulamium Park

It was a text message that alerted me this time to the demise of a tree: 'Big tree down in the Park'. Donato took photographs of it.

Here are all four of the photographs he took. I find them moving.

The demise of a horsechestnut tree in Verulamium Park

Ver valley ash

John Pritchard and I met at Ver Valley Society meetings. John manages the Society's Twitter account, keeping us in touch with what is happening along the banks of the River Ver. Here are his photographs of a huge ash tree that looks as if it was wrenched apart but its branches cushioned its landing.

We can see that birds had used its trunk as a home – perhaps many generations of birds.

A fallen ash tree in the River Ver valley between Gorhambury and Redbournbury

Cedar at St Marys Redbourn

On Sunday 10th December 2017, a branch fell from the cedar in the churchyard of St Marys, Redbourn. Pauline Ridgewell sent photographs and tells us, 'It was just before the 9.30 am service started, while we were ringing the bells. It was quite a loud crashing sound as we heard it over the sound of the bells.

Cedar at St Marys Redbourn in December 2017 Photo by Pauline Ridgewell)

'One of the bell ringers had earlier walked directly beneath it. He had a lucky escape.

'I believe three branches came down but not all at the same time.'

The cedars at St Peters, St Michaels, the Abbey and St Marys, Redbourn each add to the beauty of their churchyards. All are veteran trees. Each is having to be closely watched.

Ash of Ash Grove

At 6.30pm on a dark October Saturday evening in 2017, Cathy Honey and her husband were in the kitchen of their home in Ash Grove, Wheathampstead. They heard a swish and felt a change in pressure. They heard and felt no more than that: no bang, no crash. 'It was like a flying saucer landing,' said Cathy. There, within a few feet of where they were standing, was the full length of the ash tree that had been on the roadside verge but was now in their garden. In its fall, the tree had demolished the fence and the back of the Honeys' garage.

The ash tree in Ash Grove lying in the Honey's garden

Hertfordshire County Council officers came in response to the Honeys' call. They gave advice and, Cathy said, are reviewing the safety of other trees in Ash Grove. Several of the trees are huge, so do get to see them before they are 'made safe'.

We do so hate it and complain when our trees are taken down or cut back, but the consequences of leaving trees unmanaged can be catastrophic. The Honeys narrowly escaped a dreadful fate.

Cathy adds, 'We look at the empty space now and we, and our neighbours, miss the majestic presence of the ash tree. Also, we certainly noticed a difference during this hot Summer. Without the cooling shade of the tree, our bedrooms and patio got incredibly hot.

'My dad said, 'Think of all the oxygen that tree produced.' Sadly no longer.'

I regret that we did not take a photograph of the ash in Ash Grove when it was at the height of its glory, but I do have ones that show its size in 2012, sometime after being pruned back.

The ash tree in Ash Grove in October 2012

Bark of the ash tree in Ash Grove in October 2012

CHAPTER THIRTEEN

New to the book

Hospital cedar

The only thing that is 'new' about the cedar outside what used to be the Nurses Home at the Waverley Road entrance to St Albans City Hospital is that I had not noticed it before. I was sitting at the bus stop waiting for a bus, lifted my eyes and realised I was looking at a lovely tree. It is what you need outside a hospital. Many people must arrive in pain or anxiety or leave after shocking news and have to sit waiting for a bus. It is good to have our tall cedar to calm and encourage us.

Amwell's oldest ash

'Have you seen our ash tree?' I was asked, as we sat in the garden of a mutual friend. Donato and I arranged to see the ash. It has the Wow! factor. It is a great beast of a tree in a hedge between a garden and a footpath.

Left:
Cedar at the
Waverley Road
entrance to St
Albans City
Hospital

Right:
Amwells's ancient
ash: the beast's
base

In the garden, we see its massive crown spreading fully and symmetrically, but with different shades of green on the leaves on one side of the crown compared to the other. I wonder what causes the different shades of green. Perhaps it is simply the differing amounts of direct sunlight, but I have not seen such a marked effect before. It certainly adds character to an already imposing tree.

There is no need to be in the garden to experience the thrill of the tree: we can do that from the footpath. It runs from the first small open triangle you come to as you leave Nomansland and Ferrers Lane to go north on Down Green Lane, towards the Elephant and Castle pub in Amwell. There is a track from the right-hand corner of the triangle and the footpath is soon on the left. At the height of Summer in 2018, there were nettles on either side of the footpath, but well enough back not to be a problem. Do go the 30 paces along the footpath to see the ash tree. You will be impressed by the diameter of the trunk – the width of a tall man's length. If we call the length 80 inches, remember that circumference is $2\pi r$, and apply the Woodland Trust rule of thumb (an inch in girth every year), we get a girth of 80x3, which is approximately 250 inches, and the age of the tree, therefore, about 250 years. Our tree is a Georgian tree, about the same age as the Bishop's venerable pagoda tree.

Look up into the crown of the tree and marvel at the branching and canopy.

While you are seeking the Amwell ash, enjoy the view into a wilderness of woodland that can be seen alongside the track from the open triangle. It is part of Nomansland Common north of Ferrers Lane.

Chalkdrawers ash

I was on a walk that took us from Sleapshyde, over the North Orbital A414, through the countryside and on towards Colney Heath, when I noticed a particularly large horizontal branch of a long-ago laid tree. We immediately came out on to Roestock Lane at the Chalkdrawers Arms car park and I was able to see the tree from its other side. I was astounded by the bulk of the tree and asked Donato to go back with me. You can see from his photograph just how massive it is.

The Chalkdrawers Arms is closed now but was once a busy community pub. It is not far along Roestock Lane from Colney Heath High Street. Savour Donato's photograph. Who knows what the fate of our tree will be as the use of the site changes.

A lone field maple, and St Vincent Drive green

Alison Metcalfe saw in the Civic Society newsletter that I was updating my book and told me of a tree she found interesting in Haig Close, in the

Chalkdrawers
Arms contorted
ash

Cunningham area. I went to find it. It is a field maple with a girth of 70 inches. If it is 70 years old is must be at least as old as the houses around it and perhaps was a hedge tree that was allowed to escape.

eld maple as
as the houses
und it

I asked a local lad if he or other youngsters ever climbed it but he said no. Perhaps the stern 'no ball games' sign opposite deters them from feeling they are allowed any fun.

Alison also drew my attention to a green on St Vincent Drive. There are bird cherries, cockspur thorn, limes and maples set out in the most attractive way. What a spread of colour there must be in Spring and Autumn.

Again, I liked the thought of children playing in the trees. Under the limes there is a den carpeted in gold.

The street trees on Cell Barnes Lane, Drakes Drive – in fact all about that Cunningham area – make a huge difference to its feel.

A den carpeted in gold

Young *Ginkgo biloba* trees in Victoria Street

On the very last page, within the chapter 'Trees and the future', I expressed the hope that the avenue of trees in Victoria Street could be revived.

My hopes are in the process of being fulfilled: *Ginkgo biloba* trees have been planted on either side of the lower parts of Victoria Street. They are lovely trees with pretty leaves, graceful branching and bold gold Autumn colour.

The trees are young but will grow to a great height. *Ginko biloba* is a most robust species. It survived the bombing of Hiroshima and I am sure will survive the traffic and pavement-pounding it will be subjected to in Victoria Street.

Ginkgo biloba trees in Victoria Street

Remarkable trees at Mackerye End

250-year-old *Ginkgo biloba*

Mackerye End is within St Albans District, northeast of Harpenden, about half a mile from Batford in the general direction of Gustard Wood.

Grab any chance you get to walk past the estate or attend an NGS Open Garden Day. There is a spectacular white-flowering Cornus tree, a *Ginkgo biloba* dating back to the 1750s, two magnificent tulip trees, a bushy old mulberry tree and the atmospheric ancient sweet chestnut trees – see overleaf.

There are various new plantings including young oak trees, a box maze and other box hedges, a parterre and a dwarf orchard enclosed by yew hedges. All are set in our lovely Hertfordshire rural landscape, with the elegant architecture of Mackerye End House as an immediate backdrop.

Tulip trees at Mackerye House

The most remarkable trees in St Albans District

The sweet chestnut trees at Mackerye End are remarkable for their history, their antiquity, their beauty - and for the emotions they invoke.

They are sweet chestnuts, *Castanea sativa*, a beautiful tree, the grooves of its bark snaking upwards to a full crown of spreading branches and large, glossy, serrated-edged leaves.

Two of the trees 'are thought to have been planted around 1603'. Yes, they are sweet chestnuts, and they are more than 400 years old.

They 'are believed to be' a gift from the King of Spain. Which King of Spain would that be? It was about the time of the end of the reign of our Elizabeth I. Could Philip II, who launched the Armada against England, who had been husband of Elizabeth I's elder sister Bloody Mary, still be living? No, he died in 1598. Who followed him? He was succeeded by his 20-year-old son, Philip III. So, our trees are believed to be a gift from a man in his twenties, King of Spain, King of Portugal, King of Naples and Sicily, Duke of Milan, lord of the Seventeen Provinces of the Netherlands, and Emperor of the Spanish Territories that were on every continent then known – including the Philippines, named for his father.

They are believed to have been a gift to celebrate the accession of our King James I of England, King James VI of Scotland.

Why would such a gift be planted at Mackerye End? Who knows.

Here are photographs of one of the trees at Mackerye End.

The tree shares its base with a young holly

One of the 400-year-old sweet chestnut at Mackerye End

I like it that the tree seems content to share its root space with a young holly. After more than 400 years, our tree is not the towering beauty it must have been at its zenith but has a beauty of its own, and radiates an uncanny mixture of energy, optimism – and mystery.

What a finale to be able to leave you with.

References

Bean, W.J., *Trees and Shrubs Hardy in the British Isles*, Vol 3., 8th Edn, 1970, 1980 impression.

Billings, Tony, *The Camp: A Local St Albans History*, published by the author, 2002.

Burley, Peter, Elliott, Michael and Watson, Harvey, *The Battles of St Albans*, Pen & Sword, 2007.

Coombs, Vic, *Seek a Tree in Verulamium Park*, published by the author, 2004.

Corbett, James, *A History of St Albans*, Phillimore & Co. Ltd, 1997.

Crook, W.G.S., Some account of Redbourn Past and Present, *Hertfordshire Countryside*, Vol.24, issue No. 130, February 1970.

Dunk, Geoff, *Around St Albans with Geoff Dunk*, St Albans and Hertfordshire Architectural and Archaeological Society (SAHAAS), 1985.

Fookes, Michael, *Made in St Albans: Ten Town Trails*, published by the author, 1997.

Freeman, Ian, The Baa-Lamb Trees at Harpenden, *Hertfordshire's Past*, No. 3, Autumn 1977.

Gibbs, A.E., *The Corporation Records*, St Albans, 1890.

Grey, Edwin, *Rothamsted Experimental Station: Reminiscences, Tales and Anecdotes of the Laboratories, Staff and Experimental Fields, 1822-1922*, published by the author in 1922.

Hebditch, Felicity, *A History of Victoria Square*, produced by Irish Life Assurance plc, 1993.

Hertfordshire Environmental Forum, *The State of Biodiversity in Hertfordshire 1992–2002*, Hertfordshire Biological Records Centre, 2003.

Hertfordshire & Middlesex Trust for Nature Conservation (HMTNC), *Verulamium Nature Trail*, 1982.

Hooper, Max, 'The History of Hooper's Hedgerow Hypothesis', a British Naturalists' Association lecture given by Dr Hooper when presented with the Peter Scott Memorial Award 2004 at Hallsannery Field Centre, Bideford, Devon.

James, Trevor J., *Flora of Hertfordshire*, Hertfordshire Natural History Society, 2009.

Lipscombe, Margaret and Stokes, Jon of The Tree Council, '*Trees and How to Grow Them*', Think Books, 2008.

Middleditch, Michael, *The St Albans Map Guide*, Michael Graham Publications, 2008.

Miles, Archie, *The Trees that Made Britain*, BBC Books, 2006.

Mitchell, Alan and Coombes, Allen, *The Garden Tree*, Weidenfield & Nicolson, 1998.

Mitchell, Alan, *A Field Guide to the Trees of Britain and Northern Europe*, Collins, 1976.

Moody, Brian, Ed., *A History in All Men's Lives*, St Albans and Hertfordshire Architectural and Archaeological Society, 1999.

Niblett, Rosalind, *Verulamium: The Roman City of St Albans*, Tempus Publishing Ltd, 2001.

Niblett, Rosalind, *Roman Hertfordshire*, Tempus Publishing Ltd, 2000.

Nowak, D.J., McHale, P.J., Ibarra, M., Crane, D., Stevens, J.C. and Luley, C.J. (1998) 'Modelling the effects or urban vegetation on air pollution', in Gryning, S. and Chaumerliac, N. (Eds) *Air Pollution Modelling and Its Application XII*, Plenum Press, New York, 399–407.

Powe, Neil A. and Willis, Kenneth G., 'Mortality and Morbidity Benefits of Air Pollution Absorption by Woodland', report to the Forestry Commission, December 2002.

Rackham, Oliver, *Woodlands*, Collins, 2006.

Rowe, Anne and Williamson, Tom, *Hertfordshire a landscape history*, Hertfordshire Publications, 2013.

Shaw, S.G., *History of Verulam & St Albans*, 1815.

Sterry, Paul, *Collins Complete Guide to British Trees*, HarperCollins, 2007.

Thomas, Peter A., *Trees, Their Natural History* Second Edition, 2014.

Tomkins, M., The story of the oaks of Hertfordshire, *Hertfordshire Countryside*, Vol.20, issue No. 80, November 1965.

Toms, Elsie, *The Story of St Albans*, 1962.

Tudge, Colin *The Secret Life of Trees: How They Live and Why They Matter*, Penguin, 2005.

Wilks, J.H., *Trees of the British Isles in History & Legend*, Frederick Muller, 1972.

Wittering, W. O., Topiary in Hertfordshire, *Hertfordshire Countryside*, Vol.22, issue No. 103, November 1967.

Index

Entries in **bold** type are more substantial in the main text than those not in bold type.